TALKING TEXTS

Oscar: The Importance of Being Wilde

Jeremy Hunter and John McRae

Penguin English

PENGUIN BOOKS

Published by the Penguin Group
Penguin Books Ltd, 27 Wrights Lane, London W8 5TZ, England
Penguin Books USA Inc., 375 Hudson Street, New York, New York 10014, USA
Penguin Books Australia Ltd, Ringwood, Victoria, Australia
Penguin Books Canada Ltd, 10 Alcorn Avenue, Toronto, Ontario, Canada M4Y 3B2
Penguin Books (NZ) Ltd, 182–190 Wairau Road, Auckland 10, New Zealand
Penguin Books Ltd, Registered Offices: Harmondsworth, Middlesex, England

First published 1991
10 9 8 7 6 5 4 3 2 1

Filmset in Monophoto Photina and Helvetica
Printed in England by Clays Ltd, St Ives plc

Dedicated to

PAMELA FALANGA

Colleague and friend
An unforgettable Lady Bracknell

Contents

Introduction

The Penguin 'Talking Texts' series is intended as a study aid for students of English language, and of English literature, who want to experience the sound, the imagination and the expression of writers of literature. The unique feature of the Penguin 'Talking Texts' series is the importance placed on the actual listening. Experience has shown that simultaneous reading and listening is a valuable way into the comprehension and the enjoyment of literary texts. Students are invited to approach the written word in the same way as they would attend a theatre or cinema performance.

Listening – a question of focus

Any listening material which is *more* than a communication of information (unlike a news bulletin, or most listening comprehension material) invites the listener to engage imaginatively with what is heard. The material is representational rather than referential: it *shows* rather than simply *telling*. With representational materials the receiver goes beyond comprehension of the basic meaning of what is heard (although that is, of course, a vital step), in order to engage with the communicative intention, the tone, the implications, the subtext, the interplay of voices and of voice and silence, the intonation and rhythm, of the spoken text.

How to listen

You can listen to the texts in many ways, and you should try as many ways as possible.

All the way through
This gives you the whole effect, and you can listen while following the texts in the book, or just for the sound. This *global* listening can be done at any time – before, during or after any class work on the texts.

Text by text

This more *intensive* way of listening can be taken when you want to listen more closely to single items – while you are working on the accompanying exercises or just to build up your understanding of how the texts link with each other.

Single texts

This kind of listening helps you to deepen your understanding of one text, concentrating on single words or phrases, rhythm, rhyme, intonation (which you might want to imitate, discuss or comment on), characterisation and effects. *Interpretation* is important here; does the performer on the cassette interpret the text the way you would? Feel free to criticize and evaluate aspects of the performance, and to try out your own performance at any time!

In class/on your own

It is perfectly possible to use the Penguin 'Talking Texts' series for individual study and appreciation of literature. Naturally in a classroom situation everyone can listen at the same time, especially if everyone is working on the same text or discussing the same topic. But the advantage of everyone having a cassette is that you can listen to a text or texts at any time on your personal stereo or 'Walkman' and different groups in the same class can work on different parts of the performance at the same time, without problems.

Listening activities

Here are some of the specific kinds of listening activity you will find in the text:

– for information
– for gist
– intensive listening
– for main points
– for interpretation
– to check predictions/intuitions
– to identify words
– to identify speakers
– to identify tone and attitude
– to pick out specific items
– for pronunciation
– to initiate discussion

Most of the texts are accompanied by three sections, Listening, Reading and Discussion, so that the listening activity is always developed for a fuller understanding of the text, as well as relating to the performance of the text. Some of the very brief texts which link the longer texts have just one or two questions – they serve as a bridge, a stimulus between aspects of the subject.

How the cassette relates to the book

The texts are printed in the order in which they are performed, so that you can follow the development of the presentation, moment by moment. You can stop listening and look more closely at a single text, and work through the questions and tasks exactly as you wish.

The exercises accompanying each text are designed to help clarify problems like vocabulary, syntax, effect, and so on. They are principally intended to add to your enjoyment of the performance, by helping your understanding and giving you points to ponder and possibly discuss.

Character is important in how you react to the readings – very often a character reveals himself or herself in his or her own words, and the audience realizes the character's qualities and defects. Feel free to judge the characters – not just to understand their words, but also what the words reveal about them!

Because the performance might arouse your interest in Oscar Wilde or the texts, a few very brief details are given at the back of the book. Use these, if you wish, as a starting point to find out more about, or read more of, a text you have found particularly interesting.

Every time you listen to the texts you will understand them a little differently. When working with the book, the whole performance will take on a clearer shape in your own mind, as the sounds you hear give more and more meaning to the texts you read. The listening is the first part of the enjoyment of exploring these texts. But it is also the last, and *lasting*, part of the pleasure of the performance – a theatrical event, a 'show' you can listen to over and over again, act along with, and even perform yourself.

Oscar: The Importance of Being Wilde

In the 1850s the Crown Prince of Sweden was called Oscar. He later became King Oscar. Our Oscar, born in 1854, was not a prince. His father was a doctor, an Irishman, but was famous enough to become doctor to royalty. In 1862 William Wilde was honoured by the Court of Sweden. Two years later Queen Victoria made him a knight: Sir William Wilde.

The name Oscar is not fashionable in Britain in the twentieth century – because of Oscar Wilde. He represented something people considered terrible in the 1890s – he was unconventional: Wilde openly condemned the hypocrisy of British society in the 1880s and 1890s, and his homosexuality led to a prison sentence in 1895. For some years afterwards homosexuals were often called 'Oscars'. But Wilde did not feel that he had to apologize for his way of life.

Oscar Wilde made his career as a writer. He did not write what the majority of British readers expected to read. And Oscar was intolerant of adverse criticism. He refused to conform to the values of late-Victorian England, but he wished to be appreciated as an artist. He believed that the beauty of art was the most important thing in life. His last and greatest public success came with the play *The Importance of Being Earnest*, in 1895. 'Earnest' is an adjective which means serious and solemn, but its sound is exactly the same as the name Ernest. Our title echoes Oscar's famous punning title. His name was Wilde, but the adjective 'wild' can describe a person who is angry – who cannot be restrained or forced to 'conform' – or a person who is very enthusiastic about something. Among the following texts you will find examples of Oscar Wilde's wildness, in the form of anger, enthusiasm and frustration. This often took the form of lecturing against established opinions that he believed were wrong.

But the works of Oscar Wilde offer much more than this: for example, a scholarly command of language – his early works have a distinct echo of earlier forms of English. But above all, Wilde's writing is full of wit, humour and gentle laughter – generally appreciated as much today as when it was written. We hope you enjoy this 'performance'.

1. Quotations

The artist is the creator of beautiful things.

(Preface to *The Picture of Dorian Gray*)

Pleasure is the only thing one should live for.

(*Phrases and Philosophies for the Use of the Young*)

I have nothing to declare except my genius.

(attributed, upon his arrival in New York, 2 January 1882)

There is no such thing as a moral or an immoral book. Books are well written, or badly written. That is all.

(Preface to *The Picture of Dorian Gray*)

Wickedness is a myth invented by good people to account for the curious attractiveness of others.

(*Phrases and Philosophies for the Use of the Young*)

A man cannot be too careful in the choice of his enemies.

(*The Picture of Dorian Gray*)

Experience is the name everyone gives to their mistakes.

(*Lady Windermere's Fan*)

We can forgive a man for making a useful thing as long as he does not admire it. The only excuse for making a useless thing is that one admires it intensely.

(Preface to *The Picture of Dorian Gray*)

All art is quite useless.

(Preface to *The Picture of Dorian Gray*)

In aesthetic criticism, attitude is everything.

(*The Truth of Masks*)

Listening

Here are some short sayings by Oscar Wilde. Which do you like best? Can you say why?

Reading

a) Try to explain the double meaning of 'declare' in the third quotation. Remember that Wilde was talking to a customs officer.

b) Rewrite the final quotation, using some or all of the following words and phrases:

point of view	beautiful
commentary	based upon
the be all and end all	perception

c) Look up the following words in your dictionary:

contradiction	paradox
epigram	pun

Now see which you can relate to any of these quotations. For example, what about the title *The Truth of Masks* (see the last quotation)?

Discussion

d) What do *you* think is the value of art? Consider music and painting as well as literature. Is it possible for art to be 'immoral', in your opinion?

e) How would you define 'experience?' Does the common English phrase 'to learn from (bitter) experience' help you?

2. The Decay of Lying (1889)

Art never expresses anything but itself. It has an independent life, just as Thought has, and develops purely on its own lines. It is not necessarily realistic in an age of realism, nor spiritual in an age of faith. So far from being the creation of its time, it is usually in direct opposition to it, and the only history that it preserves for us is the history of its own progress. Sometimes it returns upon its footsteps, and revives some antique form, as happened in the archaistic movement of late Greek Art, and in the pre-Raphaelite movement in our own day. At other times it entirely anticipates its age, and produces in one century work that it takes another century to understand, to appreciate, and to enjoy. In no case does it reproduce its age. To pass from the art of a time to the time itself is the great mistake that all historians commit.

The second doctrine is this. All bad art comes from returning to Life and Nature, and elevating them into ideals. Life and Nature may sometimes be used as part of Art's rough material, but before they are of any real service to Art they must be translated into artistic conventions. The moment Art surrenders its imaginative medium it surrenders everything. (. . .)

At twilight nature becomes a wonderfully suggestive effect, and is not without loveliness, though perhaps its chief use is to illustrate quotations from the poets.

Listening

As you listen to this extract from an essay, try to decide what Wilde thinks Art expresses, and what bad art comes from. The next time you listen, try to decide what Art is *not*.

Reading

a) Are the following statements true or false, according to Wilde?

Art is always unrealistic in a period dominated by realistic thought.

Art is never spiritual in a period dominated by religious thought.

Art always presents a picture or impression of a different period from that in which it was created.

Find evidence in the first paragraph which supports your answers. Pay particular attention to adverbs and adverbial phrases.

b) What is the 'second doctrine' (line 13) in your own words? Should artists reject 'Life and Nature' completely? Try to rewrite this paragraph in one sentence.

Discussion

c) Write a few lines – possibly even a poem! – about the moon. What images does the moon create in your mind? Do you perhaps know some songs which refer to the moon? When you have finished your composition, read the following quotations from Oscar Wilde's play *Salomé*:

> She is like a woman rising from a tomb.
> She is like a little princess who wears a yellow veil, and whose feet are of silver.
> She is like a little piece of money, you would think she was a little silver flower.
> She is like a mad woman, a mad woman who is seeking everywhere for lovers. She is naked, too. (. . .) She reels through the clouds like a drunken woman.
> (. . .) the moon is like the moon, that is all.

Now comment on the word 'suggestive' in the main passage (line 19). What did the moon 'suggest' to you? Try to explain the paradox at the end of this passage.

3. *Requiescat* (1881)

Tread lightly, she is near
  Under the snow,
Speak gently, she can hear
  The daisies grow.

All her bright golden hair
  Tarnished with rust,
She that was young and fair
  Fallen to dust.

Lily-like, white as snow,
  She hardly knew
She was a woman so
  Sweetly she grew.

Coffin-board, heavy stone,
  Lie on her breast,
I vex my heart alone,
  She is at rest.

Peace, peace, she cannot hear
  Lyre or sonnet,
All my life's buried here,
  Heap earth upon it.

Listening

Try to decide, while listening, who 'she' (line 1) is and what has happened to her. Then listen again, to pick out words from the poem which confirm your answer.

Reading

a) Who is the poet speaking to?
b) How do you think the poet was related to 'she'?
c) Try to find one direct reference to 'art' in the poem. Can you also find one direct contrast which refers to 'nature'?

Discussion

d) How old do you think 'she' was? Think of some adjectives which describe the poet's feelings: for example, is he morbid, reconciled, depressed, contemplative?

4. *The Picture of Dorian Gray* (1890/91)

'You went to the Opera? You went to the Opera while Sybil Vane was lying dead in some sordid lodging? You can talk to me of other women being charming, and of Patti singing divinely, before the girl you loved has even the quiet of a grave to sleep in? Why, man, there are horrors in store for that little white body of hers!'

'Stop, Basil! I won't hear it! You must not tell me about things. What is done is done. What is past is past.'

'You call yesterday the past?'

'What has the lapse of time got to do with it? It is only shallow people who require years to get rid of an emotion. A man who is master of himself can end a sorrow as easily as he can invent a pleasure. I don't want to be at the mercy of my emotions. I want to use them, to enjoy them, and to dominate them.'

'Dorian, this is horrible! Something has changed you completely. You look exactly the same wonderful boy who, day after day, used to come down to my studio to sit for his picture. But you were simple, natural, and affectionate then. You were the most unspoiled creature in the whole world. Now, I don't know what has come over you. You talk as if your had no heart, no pity in you. It is all Harry's influence. I see that.'

'I owe a great deal to Harry, Basil: more than I owe to you. You only taught me to be vain.'

'Well, I am punished for that, Dorian – or shall be some day.'

'I don't know what you mean, Basil. I don't know what you want. What do you want?'

'I want the Dorian I used to paint.'

'Basil, you have come too late. Yesterday when I heard that Sybil Vane had killed herself –'

'Killed herself! Good heavens! is there no doubt about that?'

'My dear Basil! Surely you don't think it was a vulgar accident? Of course she killed herself.'

'How fearful.'

'No, there is nothing fearful about it. It is one of the great romantic tragedies of the age. As a rule, people who act lead the most commonplace lives. They are good husbands, or faithful wives, or something tedious. You know what I mean – middle-class virtue, and all that kind of thing. How different Sybil was! She lived her finest tragedy. She was always a heroine. The last night she played – the night you saw her – she acted badly because she had known the reality of love. When she knew its unreality, she died, as Juliet might have died. She passed again into the sphere of art. There is something of the martyr about her.'

Listening

Basil Hallward, a painter, is arguing with Dorian Gray, a friend whose portrait he has recently painted. Dorian's girlfriend – an actress called Sybil Vane – has just died.

How would you describe Basil's reactions to what Dorian tells him? Is he angry, surprised, bored, jealous or something else? Which character strikes you as more 'positive'? Can you say why?

Reading

a) Try to express in your own words what Dorian Gray says about time – past and future – in his first two speeches.

b) Why does Dorian respect Harry more than he respects Basil? Look again at Basil's previous speech. Is Dorian's judgement of Basil justified?

c) Place the following (rewritten) statements in the same order as they occur in the final paragraph of the passage.

> Actors and actresses usually have boring existences.
>
> On her final appearance she failed to act like a lover because she believed she had a real-life lover.
>
> It is not a disaster. Nowadays, suicide is an unhappy recognition of mistaken love.
>
> Most actors and actresses have dull and conventional marriages, and wish to maintain their good social reputations.
>
> Her self-sacrifice was positive from the artistic point of view, and even from the religious point of view.
>
> She was not like that: and her own life was more tragic than any of the roles she played. In herself, she was a star.
>
> When she knew her love was mistaken, she killed herself; as a character from a play by Shakespeare might have done.

Discussion

d) Remembering that Dorian Gray has rejected Sybil Vane, what do you think when he calls her suicide 'one of the great romantic tragedies of the age'?

5. *The Truth of Masks* (1885)

I think it is a pity that so many critics should have set themselves to attack one of the most important movements on the modern stage before that movement has at all reached its proper perfection. That it will do so, however, I feel as certain as that we shall require from our dramatic critics in the future higher qualifications than that they can remember Macready or have seen Benjamin Webster; we shall require of them, indeed, that they cultivate a sense of beauty. (. . .) The truths of metaphysics are the truth of masks.

Listening

This essay was first published with the title *Shakespeare and Stage Costume*. Do you find the passage optimistic or pessimistic? Which words make you think so?

Reading

a) What does Wilde dislike about modern theatre criticism?

Discussion

b) William Macready and Benjamin Webster (line 6) were both famous actors: Macready was born in 1793, retired from the stage in 1851, and died in 1873; Webster was born in 1797, retired from the stage in 1874, and died in 1882. Why do you think Wilde says (in 1885) that being able to remember these two stars is not a sufficient qualification for a dramatic critic?

Today, what would *you* think of a critic who always spoke about Marilyn Monroe (died 1962) or Laurence Olivier (retired from the stage 1974; died 1989)?

6. *The Picture of Dorian Gray* (1890/91)

'Let us go and sit in the shade. Parker has brought out the drinks, and if you stay any longer in this glare you will be quite spoiled, and Basil will never paint you again. You really must not allow yourself to become sunburnt. It would be unbecoming.'

'What can it matter?'

'It should matter everything to you, Mr Gray.'

'Why?'

'Because you have the most marvellous youth, and youth is the one thing worth having.'

'I don't feel that, Lord Henry.'

'No, you don't feel it now. Some day when you are old and wrinkled and ugly, when thought has seared your forehead with its lines, and passion branded your lips with its hideous fires, you will feel it, you will feel it terribly. Now, wherever you go, you charm the world. Will it always be so? ... You have a wonderfully beautiful face, Mr Gray. Don't frown. You have. (. . .) Ah! realize your youth while you have it. Don't squander the gold of your days, listening to the tedious, trying to improve the hopeless failure, or giving away your life to the ignorant, the common, and the vulgar. These are the sickly aims, the false ideals of our age. Live! Live the wonderful life that is in you! Let nothing be lost upon you. Be always searching for new sensations. Be afraid of nothing . . . (. . .) You are glad to have met me, Mr Gray?'

'Yes, I am glad now. I wonder shall I always be glad?'

'Always! That is a dreadful word. It makes me shudder when I hear it. Women are so fond of using it. They spoil every romance by trying to make it last for ever. It is a meaningless word, too. The only difference between a caprice and a life-long passion is that the caprice lasts a little longer.'

Listening

In this second extract from Oscar Wilde's only novel, Dorian Gray is talking to Sir Henry Wotton (the 'Harry' mentioned earlier). They are sitting in Basil Hallward's garden.

What does Sir Henry say is Dorian's greatest advantage in life? Pick out contrasts between youth and age, beauty and ugliness. How many references to time can you find?

Reading

a) Who do you think 'Parker' (line 1) is? What does Sir Henry recommend? Can you say why?

b) Match the words in the left-hand column with the definitions in the right-hand column.

glare (line 2)	spend extravagantly
unbecoming (line 4)	shake with horror
seared (line 12)	very bright light
hideous (line 13)	making less beautiful
realise (line 16)	romantic game; affair
squander (line 17)	enjoy; make the best of
shudder (line 24)	cut
caprice (line 27)	horrible; foul

c) Rewrite in your own words what Sir Henry describes as 'the sickly aims, the false ideals, of our age' (lines 19–26). Do you agree that these are mistaken social ambitions? Why, or why not?

d) Which word is 'meaningless' (line 26)?

Discussion

e) Which of the following adjectives best describe Sir Henry Wotton, in your opinion?

dangerous	innocent	witty
misanthropic	outrageous	happy
gay	cynical	flirtatious
frivolous	violent	aesthetic

7. *An Ideal Husband* (1895)

MRS CHEVELEY: I loved you, Arthur.

LORD GORING: My dear Mrs Cheveley, you have always been far too clever to know anything about love.

MRS CHEVELEY: I did love you. And you loved me. You know you loved me; and love is a very wonderful thing. I suppose that when a man has once loved a woman, he will do anything for her, except continue to love her?

LORD GORING: Yes; except that.

MRS CHEVELEY: I am tired of living abroad. I want to come back to London. I want to have a charming house here. I want to have a salon. If one could only teach the English how to talk, and the Irish how to listen, society here would be quite civilized. Besides, I have arrived at the romantic stage. When I saw you last night at the Chilterns', I knew you were the only person I had ever cared for, if I ever have cared for anybody, Arthur. And so, on the morning of the day you marry me, I will give you Robert Chiltern's letter. That is my offer. I will give it to you now, if you promise to marry me.

LORD GORING: Now?

MRS CHEVELEY: Tomorrow.

LORD GORING: Are you really serious?

MRS CHEVELEY: Yes, quite serious.

LORD GORING: I should make you a very bad husband.

MRS CHEVELEY: I don't mind bad husbands. I have had two. They amused me immensely.

LORD GORING: You mean that you amused yourself immensely, don't you?

MRS CHEVELEY: What do you know about my married life?

LORD GORING: Nothing: but I can read it like a book.

MRS CHEVELEY: What book?

LORD GORING: The Book of Numbers.

MRS CHEVELEY: Do you think it is quite charming of you to be so rude to a woman in your own house?

LORD GORING: In the case of very fascinating women, sex is a challenge, not a defence.

MRS CHEVELEY: I suppose that is meant for a compliment. My dear Arthur, women are never disarmed by compliments. Men always are. That is the difference between the two sexes.

LORD GORING: Women are never disarmed by anything, as far as I know them.

MRS CHEVELEY: Then you are going to allow your greatest friend, Robert Chiltern, to be ruined, rather than marry someone who really has considerable attractions left. I thought you would have risen to some great height of self-sacrifice, Arthur. I think you should. And the rest of your life you could spend in contemplating your own perfections.

LORD GORING: Oh! I do that as it is. And self-sacrifice is a thing that should be put down by law. It is so demoralizing to the people for whom one sacrifices oneself. They always go to the bad.

MRS CHEVELEY: As if anything could demoralize Robert Chiltern! You seem to forget that I know his real character.

LORD GORING: What you know about him is not his real character. It was an act of folly done in his youth, dishonourable, I admit, shameful, I admit, unworthy of him, I admit, and therefore – not his true character.

MRS CHEVELEY: How you men stand up for each other!

LORD GORING: How you women war against each other!

MRS CHEVELEY: I only war against one woman, against Gertrude Chiltern. I hate her. I hate her now more than ever.

LORD GORING: Because you have brought a real tragedy into her life, I suppose?

MRS CHEVELEY: Oh, there is only one real tragedy in a woman's life. The fact that her past is always her lover, and her future invariably her husband.

LORD GORING: Lady Chiltern knows nothing of the kind of life to which you are alluding.

MRS CHEVELEY: A woman whose size in gloves is seven and three-quarters never knows much about anything. You know Gertrude has always worn seven and three-quarters? That is one of the reasons why there was never any moral sympathy between us. – Well, Arthur, I suppose this romantic interview may be regarded as at an end. You admit it was romantic, don't you? For the privilege of being your wife I was ready to surrender a great prize, the climax of my diplomatic career. You decline. Very well. If Sir Robert doesn't uphold my Argentine scheme, I expose him. *Voilà tout.*

Listening

In this first example of a dramatic text, how many characters are actually named? At what point do you think the conversation becomes serious?

Reading

a) Look at the first four speeches. Do you think Lord Goring ('Arthur') loved Mrs Cheveley in the past? Does he love her now? Does *she* love *him* now?

b) Mrs Cheveley is visiting London. What does she want Lord Goring to do? What is she offering in return?

c) How many husbands has Mrs Cheveley had? Does Lord Goring wish to become her next husband? Why is Mrs Cheveley offended when Lord Goring says 'The Book of Numbers' (line 30)? ('Numbers' is the English name for the fourth part of the Bible).

Discussion

d) Which of the following nouns may be used to describe either Mrs Cheveley or Lord Goring? Decide which character may be described in this way, and quote from the text to support your answers.

aristocrat	blackmailer	defender
diplomat	divorcee	foreigner
ignoramus	scoundrel	sentimentalist
snob	tragedian	wit

Look up in your dictionary any words you do not recognise. Some of these words clearly do not apply to either character. Can you say why not?

e) Mrs Cheveley apparently strongly dislikes Sir Robert Chiltern and Lady Gertrude Chiltern, who are friends of Lord Goring. Mrs Cheveley seems to have the power to upset their lives. How important, in your opinion, are the following phrases. And what do they add to your knowledge of the characters?

about Sir Robert
Robert Chiltern's letter (line 16)
an act of folly (line 52)
a great prize (line 72)
my Argentine scheme (line 74)

about Lady Gertrude
I hate her (line 58)
her past is always her lover (line 62)
Gertrude has always worn seven and three-quarters (lines 67–
    8; in other words, she has very large hands)
never any moral sympathy between us (line 69)

f) Imagine you are Lord Goring. Write a short letter to 'your greatest friend' – Sir Robert Chiltern – warning him about what Mrs Cheveley intends to do. Remember: you know Sir Robert's secret. What is the secret? Refer to it in your letter.

8. Sonnet, On Hearing the Dies Irae Sung in the Sistine Chapel (1881)

> Nay, Lord, not thus! white lilies in the spring,
>   Sad olive-groves, or silver-breasted dove,
>   Teach me more clearly of Thy life and love
> Than terrors of red flame and thundering.
> The empurpled vines dear memories of Thee bring:
>   A bird at evening flying to its nest
>   Tells me of One who had no place of rest:
> I think it is of Thee the sparrows sing.
> Come rather on some autumn afternoon,
>   When red and brown are burnished on the leaves.
>   And the fields echo to the gleaner's song,
> Come when the splendid fullness of the moon
>   Looks down upon the rows of golden sheaves,
>   And reap Thy harvest: we have waited long.

Listening

As you listen to this poem, pick out any words which recall to you maturity, endings and death. Check your answers by listening again. What impression do you have of the poem, just from the sound of it?

Reading

a) A sonnet is a poem of fourteen lines, with a clear sequence of rhymes. Using the letters a, b, c, etc., write down the rhyme scheme of this poem. Then look at the punctuation. Can you say how it helps to divide up the poet's ideas?

b) The Sistine Chapel is a very beautiful part of St Peter's Cathedral in Rome. The Dies Irae is a part of the Roman Catholic song for the dead, the Requiem Mass, which was written in Latin. A rough translation of the first two lines is:

> The day of anger, on that day
> the world will dissolve in flames.

Which line of the poem most clearly echoes these words?

c) Oscar Wilde's reaction to the singing of the Dies Irae is given in the first four words. Try to rephrase this comment in your own words. Does the poet approve or object? Why?

d) The poet is addressing God — 'Lord' (line 1). What other words can you find in the sonnet which refer directly to God?

Discussion

e) How many colours can you find in the poem? How many plants? And how many birds? What do you think all these references to nature reveal about the poet's attitude to death?

9. *The Happy Prince* (1888)

'I am come to bid you good-bye.'

'Swallow, Swallow, little Swallow, will you not stay with me one night longer?'

'It is winter and the chill snow will soon be here. In Egypt the sun is warm on the green palm-trees, and the crocodiles lie in the mud and look lazily about them. My companions are building a nest in the Temple of Baalbec, and the pink and white doves are watching them, and cooing to each other. Dear Prince, I must leave you, but I will never forget you, and next spring I will bring you back two beautiful jewels in place of those you have given away. The ruby shall be redder than a red rose, and the sapphire shall be as blue as the great sea.'

'In the square below there stands a little match-girl. She has let her matches fall in the gutter, and they are all spoiled. Her father will beat her if she does not bring home some money, and she is crying. She has no shoes or stockings, and her little head is bare. Pluck out my eye, and give it to her, and her father will not beat her.'

'I will stay with you one night longer, but I cannot pluck out your eye. You would be quite blind then.'

'Swallow, Swallow, little Swallow, do as I command you.'

So he plucked out the Prince's other eye and darted down with it. He swooped past the match-girl, and slipped the jewel into the palm of her hand. 'What a lovely piece of glass,' cried the little girl; and she ran home, laughing. Then the Swallow came back to the Prince.

'You are blind now, so I will stay with you always.'

'No, little Swallow, you must go away to Egypt.'

'I will stay with you always.'

(. . .) *The snow came, and after the snow came the frost.* (. . .) *The poor little Swallow grew colder and colder, but he would not leave the Prince, he loved him too well. He picked up crumbs outside the baker's door when the baker was not looking, and tried to keep himself warm by flapping his wings. But at last he knew that he was going to die.*

'Good-bye, dear Prince! will you let me kiss your hand?'

'I am glad that you are going to Egypt at last, little Swallow; you have stayed too long here: but you must kiss me on the lips, for I love you.'

'It is not to Egypt that I am going; I am going to the House of Death. Death is the brother of Sleep, is he not?'

And he kissed the Happy Prince on the lips, and fell down dead at his feet. At that moment a curious crack sounded inside the statue, as if something had broken. The fact is that the leaden heart had snapped right in two. It certainly was a dreadfully hard frost.

Listening

The Happy Prince is a statue, decorated with jewels. The swallow has stopped beside the statue, on his journey to Africa for the winter. At the request of the prince, the swallow has removed some of the jewels, and given them to the poor people of the town. While listening, decide why the prince asks the swallow to stay.

Reading

a) What jewels does the swallow say he will replace? And when? Which of these gems might have been the eye of the statue, do you think?
b) Find two reasons why the swallow decides to stay with the Happy Prince.

Discussion

c) Say, in your own words, what happens at the end – and why. What is the importance of the cold weather?

10. *A Woman of No Importance* (1893)

LORD ILLINGWORTH: Well, Rachel, what is over is over. All I have got to say now is that I am very pleased with our boy. The world will know him merely as my private secretary, but to me he will be something very near, and very dear. It is a curious thing, Rachel; my life seemed to be quite complete. It was not so. It lacked something, it lacked a son. I have found my son now, I am glad I have found him.

MRS ARBUTHNOT: You have no right to claim him, or the smallest part of him. The boy is entirely mine, and shall remain mine.

LORD ILLINGWORTH: My dear Rachel, you have had him to yourself for over twenty years. Why not let me have him for a little now? He is quite as much mine as yours.

MRS ARBUTHNOT: Are you talking of the child you abandoned? Of the child who, as far as you are concerned, might have died of hunger and of want?

LORD ILLINGWORTH: You forget, Rachel, it was you who left me. It was not I who left you.

MRS ARBUTHNOT: I left you because you refused to give the child a name. Before my son was born, I implored you to marry me.

LORD ILLINGWORTH: I had no expectations then. And besides, Rachel, I wasn't much older than you were. I was only twenty-two. I was only twenty-one, I believe, when the whole thing began in your father's garden.

MRS ARBUTHNOT: When a man is old enough to do wrong he should be old enough to do right also.

LORD ILLINGWORTH: My dear Rachel, intellectual generalities are always interesting, but generalities in morals mean absolutely nothing. As for saying I left our child to starve, that, of course, is untrue and silly. My mother offered you six hundred a year. But you wouldn't take anything. You simply disappeared, and carried the child away with you.

MRS ARBUTHNOT: I wouldn't have accepted a penny from her. Your father was different. He told you, in my presence, when we were in Paris, that it was your duty to marry me.

LORD ILLINGWORTH: Oh, duty is what one expects from others, it is not what one does oneself. Of course, I was influenced by my mother. Every man is when he is young.

MRS ARBUTHNOT: I am glad to hear you say so. Gerald shall certainly not go away with you.

LORD ILLINGWORTH: What nonsense, Rachel!

MRS ARBUTHNOT: Do you think I would allow my son –

LORD ILLINGWORTH: *Our son.*

MRS ARBUTHNOT: My son – to go away with the man who spoiled my youth, who ruined my life, who has tainted every moment of my days? You don't realise what my past has been in suffering and in shame.

LORD ILLINGWORTH: My dear Rachel, I must candidly say that I think Gerald's future considerably more important than your past.

MRS ARBUTHNOT: Gerald cannot separate his future from my past.

LORD ILLINGWORTH: That is exactly what he should do. That is exactly what you should help him to do. What a typical woman you are! You talk sentimentally, and you are thoroughly selfish the whole time. But don't let us have a scene. Rachel, I want you to look at this matter from the common-sense point of view, from the point of view of what is best for our son, leaving you and me out of the question. What is our son at present? An underpaid clerk in a small Provincial Bank in a third-rate English town. If you imagine he is quite happy in such a position, you are mistaken. He is thoroughly discontented.

MRS ARBUTHNOT: He was not discontented till he met you. You have made him so.

LORD ILLINGWORTH: Of course, I made him so. Discontent is the first step in the progress of a man or a nation. But I did not leave him with a mere longing for things he could not get. No, I made him a charming offer. He jumped at it, I need hardly say. Any young man would. And now, simply because it turns out that I am the boy's own father and he my own son, you propose practically to ruin his career. That is to say, if I were a perfect stranger, you would allow Gerald to go away with me, but as he is my own flesh and blood you won't. How utterly illogical you are!

MRS ARBUTHNOT: I will not allow him to go.

LORD ILLINGWORTH: How can you prevent it? What excuse can you give to him for making him decline such an offer as mine? I won't tell him in what relation I stand to him, I need hardly say. But you daren't tell him. You know that. Look how you have brought him up.

MRS ARBUTHNOT: I have brought him up to be a good man.

LORD ILLINGWORTH: Quite so. And what is the result? You have educated him to be your judge if he ever finds you out. And a bitter, an unjust judge he will be to you. Don't be deceived, Rachel. Children begin by loving their parents. After a time they judge them. Rarely, if ever, do they forgive them.

Listening

Mrs Arbuthnot (Rachel) is an unmarried mother. She is talking to Lord Illingworth, her son's father. They have not met for many years.

In this scene can you find any points at which either character alters his/her attitude towards the other? What are they basically talking about?

Reading

a) About how old is the son? What does his father want him to do?

b) Describe in your own words the differing reactions of Lord Illingworth's mother and father before their grandson (Gerald) was born. Did Mrs Arbuthnot agree with either of Lord Illingworth's parents?

c) Do you think Mrs Arbuthnot is 'selfish' (line 51)? Why does she repeat 'my son' (lines 40, 42)? In what way is Gerald's future related to her past?

d) Is Gerald now 'discontented'? Why, or why not? (Look for adjectives in the text – but remember who uses them.)

Discussion

e) Are there any lines in this text which you would call 'epigrams?' If so, who speaks these lines? Do the epigrams make the character more attractive to you, or less?

11. *The Canterville Ghost* (1887)

... he resolved to make one final effort to assert his dignity and social position, and determined to visit the insolent young Etonians the next night in his celebrated character of 'Reckless Rupert, or the Headless Earl'.

He had not appeared in this disguise for more than seventy years; in fact, not since he had so frightened pretty Lady Barbara Modish by means of it, that she suddenly broke off her engagement with the present Lord Canterville's grandfather, and ran away to Gretna Green with handsome Jack Castletown, declaring that nothing in the world would induce her to marry into a family that allowed such a horrible phantom to walk up and down the terrace at twilight. Poor Jack was afterwards shot in a duel by Lord Canterville on Wandsworth Common, and Lady Barbara died of a broken heart at Tunbridge Wells before the year was out, so, in every way it had been a great success. It was, however, an extremely difficult 'make-up', if I may use such a theatrical expression in connection with one of the greatest mysteries of the supernatural or, to employ a more scientific term, the higher-natural world, and it took him fully three hours to make his preparations. At last everything was ready,and he was very pleased with his appearance. The big leather riding-boots that went with the dress were just a little too large for him, and he could only find one of the two horse-pistols, but on the whole, he was quite satisfied, and at a quarter past one he glided out of the wainscoting and crept down the corridor. On reaching the room occupied by the twins, which I should mention was called the Blue Bed Chamber, on account of the colour of its hangings, he found the door just ajar. Wishing to make an effective entrance, he flung it wide open, when a heavy jug of water fell right down on him, wetting him to the skin, and just missing his left shoulder by a couple of inches. At the same moment he heard stifled shrieks of laughter proceeding from the four-post bed. The shock to his nervous system was so great that he fled back to his rooms as hard as he could go, and the next day he was laid up with a severe cold. The only thing that at all consoled him in the whole affair was the fact that he had not brought his head with him, for, had he done so, the consequences might have been very serious.

Listening

The Ghost lives at Canterville Chase, a big English country house which has been sold to an American family. The young twin sons of the family go to school at Eton College.

As you listen, pick out some important words which describe the Ghost's attitude towards the Americans, especially 'the young Etonians', and vice versa. Is the tone of the passage serious or not?

Reading

a) What happened 'seventy years' ago (line 5)? And why do you think it was 'a great success' (line 14)? For whom?

b) How did the Canterville Ghost arrive at the twins' bedroom? What was the bedroom called, and why?

c) How many boots was the Ghost wearing? And how many guns did he have? What did he *not* bring?

Discussion

d) Do you think this passage would be effective on film or television? If so, would it be tense, tragic, amusing, touching or something else? How many words are actually spoken by the characters?

e) Imagine you are the ghost of Lady Barbara Modish. Write one paragraph telling your story, or describe your feelings to others in the class.

12. *Fabien dei Franchi* (1881)

The silent room, the heavy creeping shade,
   The dead that travel fast, the opening door,
   The murdered brother rising through the floor,
The ghost's white fingers on thy shoulders laid
And then the lonely duel in the glade,
   The broken swords, the stifled scream, the gore,
   The grand revengeful eyes when all is o'er, –
These things are well enough – but thou wert made
   For more august creation! frenzied Lear
   Should at thy bidding wander on the heath
   With the shrill fool to mock him, Romeo
For thee should lure his love, and desperate fear
Pluck Richard's recreant dagger from its sheath –
   Thou trumpet set for Shakespeare's lips to blow!

Listening

What do you think is Fabien dei Franchi's job? Try to identify four proper names in the sonnet. Do these help you to confirm your answer?

Reading

a) What are 'these things' (line 8)? Who is referred to as 'thou' (line 8)? What is the connection?

b) Lines 1–7 tell a story. Rewrite the story in your own words, making sure you have referred to all the situations and events mentioned in the poem. You might begin: 'The room was quiet. A dark shadow passed noiselessly. A ghost . . .' Would you like to see a play which was based upon this story? Why, or why not?

Discussion

c) Write a short letter in modern English from the poet to Fabien dei Franchi. Use no more than two short paragraphs, one saying whether you like his present work, and the other saying what changes you would like to see him make.

Why, do you think, does Fabien prefer to act in non-Shakespearean drama?

13. *The Portrait of Mr W.H.* (1889)

Who was he whose physical beauty was such that it became the very corner-stone of Shakespeare's art; the very source of Shakespeare's inspiration; the very incarnation of Shakespeare's dreams? To look upon him as simply the object of certain love-poems is to miss the whole meaning of the poems: for the art of which Shakespeare talks in the Sonnets is not the art of the Sonnets themselves, which indeed were to him but slight and secret things – it is the art of the dramatist to which he is always alluding (. . .)

It is of course evident that there must have been in Shakespeare's company some wonderful boy-actor of great beauty, to whom he intrusted the presentation of his noble heroines; for Shakespeare was a practical theatrical manager as well as an imaginative poet, and Cyril Graham had actually discovered the boy-actor's name. He was Will, or, as he preferred to call him, Willie Hughes (. . .)

The only objection I made to the theory was that the name of Willie Hughes does not occur in the list of the actors of Shakespeare's company as it is printed in the first folio.

Listening

Shakespeare wrote a series of sonnets. The first published edition was dedicated to 'Mr W.H.'

As you listen to this description of a boy, how much do you find out about him? For instance:

> when he lived
> who he influenced
> his appearance (handsome or not)
> his job
> his name

Reading

a) What effect did Mr. W.H. have on Shakespeare? Looking at the first sentence of the passage, write three sentences, in your own words, each one beginning: 'Mr W.H.'s beauty was . . .'

b) Do you find the use of the word 'slight' (line 6) surprising in any way? *Who* considers Shakespeare's sonnets to be 'slight and secret things'?

c) Referring to the text, say whether the following statements are true (T) or false (F):

Mr W.H. was the object of some of Shakespeare's sonnets.

Shakespeare's references, in the sonnets, to 'art' concern his own plays.

Shakespeare did not trust a beautiful boy to play the heroines in his plays.

Shakespeare ran a theatre company.

Willie Hughes definitely acted in the first performances of Shakespeare's plays.

Justify your answers.

d) What is the 'theory' (line 14)? Whose theory is it?

Discussion

e) The American physicist Thomas Edison said, 'Genius is 1 per cent inspiration and 99 per cent perspiration.' Many people think Shakespeare was a genius. Do you think his talent required 'inspiration'? Perhaps you have written poetry yourself. Were you 'inspired'? If so, what inspired you?

14. *Lady Windermere's Fan* (1892)

LADY WINDERMERE: You think I am a Puritan, I suppose? Well, I have something of the Puritan in me. I was brought up like that. I am glad of it. My mother died when I was a mere child. I lived always with Lady Julia, my father's elder sister, you know. She was stern to me, but she taught me what the world is forgetting, the difference that there is between what is right and what is wrong. *She* allowed of no compromise. *I* allow of none!

LORD DARLINGTON: My dear Lady Windermere!

LADY WINDERMERE: You look on me as behind the age. – Well, I am! I should be sorry to be on the same level as an age like this.

LORD DARLINGTON: You think the age very bad?

LADY WINDERMERE: Yes. Nowadays people seem to look on life as a speculation. It is not a speculation. It is a sacrament. Its ideal is love. Its purification is sacrifice.

LORD DARLINGTON: Oh, anything is better than being sacrificed.

LADY WINDERMERE: Don't say that.

LORD DARLINGTON: I do say it. I feel it – I know it (. . .) And I must say I think you are very hard on modern life, Lady Windermere. Of course there is much against it, I admit. Most women, for instance, nowadays, are rather mercenary.

LADY WINDERMERE: Don't talk about such people.

LORD DARLINGTON: Well, then, setting aside mercenary people, who, of course, are dreadful, do you think seriously that women who have committed what the world calls a fault should never be forgiven?

LADY WINDERMERE: I think they should never be forgiven.

LORD DARLINGTON: And men? Do you think that there should be the same laws for men as there are for women?

LADY WINDERMERE: Certainly!

LORD DARLINGTON: I think life too complex a thing to be settled by these hard and fast rules.

LADY WINDERMERE: If we had 'these hard and fast rules', we should find life much more simple.

LORD DARLINGTON: You allow of no exception?

LADY WINDERMERE: None!

LORD DARLINGTON: Ah, what a fascinating Puritan you are, Lady Windermere!

LADY WINDERMERE: The adjective was unnecessary, Lord Darlington.

LORD DARLINGTON: I couldn't help it. I can resist everything except temptation.

LADY WINDERMERE: You have the modern affectation of weakness.
LORD DARLINGTON: It's only an affectation. Lady Windermere.

Listening

Lord Darlington is visiting Lady Windermere on the morning of her twenty-first birthday. Does Lady Winderwere consider herself to be a 'modern' young woman? What does she say which shows her opinions?

Reading

a) Look at Lady Windermere's third speech (lines 12-14). Try to rewrite what she says. The following words and phrases may help you:

financial gamble	solemn pledge
consider	goal
perfection	subjection, surrender

b) Look at Lady Windermere's remaining speeches. What adjectives would you use to describe her attitude? Choose from the following list, adding others of your own:

angry	bad-tempered	blunt
brusque	critical	determined
dogmatic	hard	juvenile
paradoxical	playful	wilful

Say why you have rejected any of the above words.

Discussion

c) How relevant is Lady Windermere's family background, in your opinion, to her Puritanical way of thinking?
d) Which of the two characters do you find more sympathetic? Can you say why?

15. *The Soul of Man Under Socialism* (1891)

A man is called affected, nowadays, if he dresses as he likes to dress. But in doing that he is acting in a perfectly natural manner. Affectation, in such matters, consists in dressing according to the views of one's neighbour, whose views, as they are the views of the majority, will probably be extremely stupid. Or a man is called selfish if he lives in the manner that seems to him most suitable for the full realization of his own personality; if, in fact, the primary aim of his life is self-development. But this is the way in which everyone should live. Selfishness is not living as one wishes to live, it is asking others to live as one wishes to live. And unselfishness is letting other people's lives alone, not interfering with them.

Listening

As you listen to this extract from Wilde's most political essay, try to decide why the words 'affected' and 'selfish' are important.

Reading

a) Whose views are 'extremely stupid' (line 5)? Why?

Discussion

b) Do you agree with Wilde's definitions of 'selfishness' and 'un-selfishness' in the last two sentences?

c) Do you yourself always dress as you choose? And are you always true to your own personality? If not (and *no one* can truthfully answer 'yes' to both these questions), think of times when you acted different-ly. Why did you do so? An example might be going for a job interview; would *you* dress and behave normally?

16. *Sonnet to Liberty* (1881)

Not that I love thy children, whose dull eyes
See nothing save their own unlovely woe,
Whose minds know nothing, nothing care to know, –
But that the roar of thy Democracies,
Thy reign of Terror, thy great Anarchies,
Mirror my wildest passions like the sea
And give my rage a brother – ! Liberty!
For this sake only do thy dissonant cries
Delight my discreet soul, else might all kings
By bloody knout or treacherous cannonades
Rob nations of their rights inviolate
And I remain unmoved – and yet, and yet,
These Christs that die upon the barricades,
God knows it I am with them, in some things.

Listening

While listening to this sonnet, make a list of all the words of noise
and violence. Which words relate most obviously to the title?

Reading

a) 'Thy children' (line 1) are the offspring of 'Liberty', as the title
tells us. Are the children of Liberty happy? (Look at lines 1–3.)
b) The poet's 'passions' (line 6) and 'rage' (line 7) lead him to
identify with Liberty. What new thought is introduced by 'else' (line
9)?
c) Does the poet want Liberty? Or is the cost of achieving it too
great?
d) Line 13 refers to the Crucifixion. Try to rewrite lines 13 and 14 in
your own words.

Discussion

e) Do you consider the poet's last three words an anti-climax, or
are they consistent with the poem as a whole?

17. *A Woman of No Importance* (1893)

LADY HUNSTANTON: Politics are in a sad way, everywhere, I am told. They certainly are in England. Dear Mr Cardew is ruining the country. I wonder Mrs Cardew allows him. I am sure, Lord Illingworth, you don't think that uneducated people should be allowed to have votes?

LORD ILLINGWORTH: I think they are the only people who should.

MR KELVIL: Do you take no side then in modern politics, Lord Illingworth?

LORD ILLINGWORTH: One should never take sides in anything, Mr Kelvil. Taking sides is the beginning of sincerity, and earnestness follows shortly afterwards, and the human being becomes a bore. However, the House of Commons really does very little harm. You can't make people good by Act of Parliament – that is something.

MR KELVIL: You cannot deny that the House of Commons has always shown great sympathy with the sufferings of the poor.

LORD ILLINGWORTH: That is its special vice. That is the special vice of the age. One should sympathise with the joy, the beauty, the colour of life. The less said about life's sores the better, Mr Kelvil.

MR KELVIL: Still our East End is a very important problem.

LORD ILLINGWORTH: Quite so. It is the problem of slavery. And we are trying to solve it by amusing the slaves.

Listening

The setting is a house-party in Norfolk. Two of Lady Hunstanton's guests are Lord Illingworth and Mr Kelvil, who is an elected Member of Parliament. While listening, try to find words which refer to deprivation, a poor standard of living and declining social standards.

Reading

a) Who do you think Mr and Mrs Cardew are?
b) Is Lord Illingworth sympathetic towards poor people – particularly in the East End of London? How can you tell?

Discussion

c) Looking at the last sentence, try to say why Lord Illingworth agrees or disagrees with the policy of the House of Commons. What do *you* think of his earlier assertion that 'One should never take sides in anything' (line 7)? What is the opposite of 'taking sides'?

18. *The Importance of Being Earnest* (1895)

ALGERNON: Now, go on. Why are you Ernest in town and Jack in the country?

JACK: My dear Algy, I don't know whether you will be able to understand my real motives. You are hardly serious enough. When one is placed in the position of guardian, one has to adopt a very high moral tone on all subjects. It's one's duty to do so. And as a high moral tone can hardly be said to conduce very much to either one's health or one's happiness, in order to get up to town I have always pretended to have a younger brother of the name of Ernest, who lives in the Albany, and gets into the most dreadful scrapes. That, my dear Algy, is the whole truth pure and simple.

ALGERNON: The truth is rarely pure and never simple. Modern life would be very tedious if it were either, and modern literature a complete impossibility!

JACK: That wouldn't be at all a bad thing.

ALGERNON: Literary criticism is not your forte, my dear fellow. Don't try it. You should leave that to people who haven't been at a University. They do it so well in the daily papers. What you really are is a Bunburyist. I was quite right in saying you were a Bunburyist. You are one of the most advanced Bunburyists I know.

JACK: What on earth do you mean?

ALOERNON: You have invented a very useful younger brother called Ernest, in order that you may be able to come up to town as often as you like. I have invented an invaluable permanent invalid called Bunbury, in order that I may be able to go down into the country whenever I choose. If it wasn't for Bunbury's extraordinary bad health, for instance, I wouldn't be able to dine with you at Willis's tonight, for I have been really engaged to Aunt Augusta for more than a week.

JACK: I haven't asked you to dine with me anywhere tonight.

ALGERNON: I know. You are absurdly careless about sending out invitations. It is very foolish of you. Nothing annoys people so much as not receiving invitations.

JACK: You had much better dine with your Aunt Augusta.

ALGERNON: I haven't the smallest intention of doing anything of the kind. To begin with, I dined there on Monday, and once a week is quite enough to dine with one's own relations. In the second place, whenever I do dine there I am always sent down with either no woman at all, or two. In the third place, I know perfectly well whom

she will place me next to, tonight. She will place me next to Mary
Farquhar, who always flirts with her own husband across the
dinner-table. That is not very pleasant. Indeed, it is not even decent
. . . and that sort of thing is enormously on the increase. The amount
of women in London who flirt with their own husbands is perfectly
scandalous. It looks so bad. It is simply washing one's clean linen in
public. Besides, now that I know you to be a confirmed Bunburyist I
naturally want to talk to you about Bunburying. I want to tell you
the rules.

Listening

As you listen to this scene, try to decide how old Algernon and Jack
are, and what their relationship might be.

Reading

a) Is this the beginning of the conversation? How can you tell?
b) A 'guardian' (line 5) is a person given responsibility by a court of
law for the upbringing of a child. Does Jack take this role seriously?
Explain in your own words the existence, or otherwise, of Ernest.
c) Has Jack attended university? What is Algernon's opinion of literary journalists? Have *they* attended university?
d) Give at least two reasons why Algernon wants Jack to take him
for dinner at Willis's.

Discussion

e) The English phrase 'to wash one's dirty linen in public' means to
make other people aware of something unpleasant in your own life.
Try to explain why Algernon describes Mary Farquhar's behaviour
as 'washing one's *clean* linen in public' (lines 45–6).
f) 'Earnest' is an adjective meaning solemn and serious. Is Algernon
'earnest'? If not, what adjectives would you use to describe him?

19. *The Picture of Dorian Gray* (1890/91)

He looked round, and saw the knife that had stabbed Basil Hallward. He had cleaned it many times, till there was no stain left upon it. It was bright, and glistened. As it had killed the painter, so it would kill the painter's work, and all that that meant. It would kill the past and when that was dead he would be free. It would kill this monstrous soul-life, and, without its hideous warnings, he would be at peace. He seized the thing, and stabbed the picture with it.

There was a cry heard, and a crash. The cry was so horrible in its agony that the frightened servants woke, and crept out of their rooms. Two gentlemen, passing in the Square below, stopped, and looked up at the great house. They walked on till they met a policeman, and brought him back. The man rang the bell several times, but there was no answer. Except for a light in one of the top windows, the house was all dark. After a time, he went away and stood in an adjoining portico, and watched.

'Whose house is that, constable?' asked the elder of the two gentlemen.

'Mr Dorian Gray's, sir,' answered the policeman.

They looked at each other, as they walked away, and sneered. One of them was Sir Henry Ashton's uncle.

Inside, in the servants' part of the house, the half-clad domestics were talking in low whispers to each other. Old Mrs Leaf was crying and wringing her hands. Francis was as pale as death.

After about a quarter of an hour, he got the coachman and one of the footmen and crept upstairs. They knocked, but there was no reply. They called out. Everything was still. Finally, after vainly trying to force the door, they got on the roof, and dropped down on the balcony. The windows yielded easily; their bolts were old.

When they entered they found, hanging on the wall, a splendid portrait of their master as they had last seen him, in all the wonder of his exquisite youth and beauty. Lying on the floor was a dead man, in evening dress, with a knife in his heart. He was withered, wrinkled, and loathsome of visage. It was not till they had examined the rings that they recognised who it was.

Listening

Dorian Gray has lived a life of pleasure for many years, without looking any older. He keeps his picture, painted by Basil Hallward, in a room at the top of his house. The man in the picture – Dorian Gray himself – now looks very old and ugly. This is the end of the story.

When you listen for the first time, try to identify exactly what happens. Then listen again, and decide which words in the passage help to create an atmosphere of violence and suspense.

Reading

a) What happened to Basil Hallward?
b) Why does Dorian Gray stab the picture?
c) Which of the following words best describe the servants?

agitated	apprehensive	convulsive
delirious	efficient	observant
partly dressed	resplendent	scornful
sleepy	talkative	terrified

d) How many people are outside the house? What do they do? How many people enter the upstairs room?

Discussion

e) Write two newspaper reports explaining what has happened to Dorian Gray and to his picture, one for a 'serious' paper, the other for a popular 'sensational' paper.
f) Do you think that youth and good looks are important for success?

20. *Taedium Vitae* (1881)

> To stab my youth with desperate knives, to wear
> This paltry age's gaudy livery,
> To let each base hand filch my treasury,
> To mesh my soul within a woman's hair,
> And be mere Fortune's lackeyed groom, – I swear
> I love it not! these things are less to me
> Than the thin foam that frets upon the sea,
> Less than the thistledown of summer air
> Which hath no seed: better to stand aloof
> Far from these slanderous fools who mock my life
> Knowing me not, better the lowliest roof
> Fit for the meanest hind to sojourn in,
> Than to go back to that hoarse cave of strife
> Where my white soul first kissed the mouth of sin.

Listening

What words or phrases link this poem to the previous text? Is the
subject matter the same, or different?

Reading

a) The following five phrases represent, very roughly, five things
the poet does not like – 'I love it not' (line 6). Try to put them in the
same order as they appear in lines 1–5:

> dressing in clothes which his contemporaries like
> getting involved in romance with girls
> being a servant of destiny
> violently or recklessly misspending his youth
> permitting bad people to deprive him of his money

b) How important are these things to the poet now? Refer in particular to lines 6–9.

c) Who might the 'slanderous fools' (line 10) be?

d) Does the poet intend to return to the 'cave of strife' (line 13)?
Find reasons and justifications for your answer.

Discussion

e) The poet is wearied with life. Find as many reasons for this as you can. Do you share any of these feelings? If so, how much is this motivated by regret for the past?

21. *Letter to Lord Alfred Douglas* (1893)

My own Boy, Your sonnet is quite lovely, and it is a marvel that those red rose-leaf lips of yours should have been made no less for music of song than for madness of kisses. Your slim gilt soul walks between passion and poetry. I know Hyacinthus, whom Apollo loved so madly, was you in Greek days.

Discussion

a) If a friend of yours sent you a poem, and you liked it, how would you reply?
b) In your opinion, is the language of this letter exaggerated, frivolous, matter-of-fact, disgusting or something else? Can you say why?

22. *Transcript of the First Trial* (1895)

'Why should a man of your age address a boy nearly twenty years younger as "My own Boy"?'

'I was fond of him. I have always been fond of him.'

'Do you adore him?'

'No, but I have always liked him. I think it is a beautiful letter. It is a poem. I was not writing an ordinary letter. You might as well cross-examine me as to whether *King Lear* or a sonnet of Shakespeare was proper.'

'Apart from art, Mr Wilde?'

'I cannot answer apart from art.'

'Suppose a man who was not an artist had written this letter, would you say it was a proper letter?'

'A man who was not an artist could not have written that letter.'

'Why?'

'Because nobody but an artist could write it. He certainly could not write the language unless he were a man of letters.'

'I can suggest, for the sake of your reputation, that there is nothing very wonderful in this "red rose-leaf lips of yours"?'

'A great deal depends on the way it is read.'

'"Your slim gilt soul walks between passion and poetry." Is that a beautiful phrase?'

'Not as you read it, Mr Carson. You read it very badly.'

'I do not profess to be an artist, and when I hear you give evidence, I am glad I am not.'

Listening

Alfred Douglas's father, the Marquess of Queensbury, wrote in 1895 that Oscar Wilde was 'posing' as a homosexual. Queensbury was arrested and put on trial. Queensbury's defence lawyer, Carson, asked Wilde about the above letter to Alfred Douglas.

As you listen to this scene from real life, try to decide what Wilde's attitude is towards Carson's questions.

Reading

a) Which words does Wilde use that contrast with 'adore' (line 4)?

b) Explain in your own words what Wilde says about the works of Shakespeare.

Discussion

c) Do you find Wilde's responses convincing?

d) Do you agree with Carson's final speech? Why is Carson 'glad' that he himself is not 'an artist'?

23. *Panthea* (1881)

> O we are wearied of this sense of guilt,
> Wearied of pleasure's paramour despair,
> Wearied of every temple we have built,
> Wearied of every right, unanswered prayer,
> For man is weak; God sleeps; and heaven is high;
> One fiery-coloured moment: one great love; and lo! we die.

Listening

As you listen to this verse from a much longer poem – the title denotes the embodiment of all the classical gods – see how many religious references you can find.

Reading

a) What is wrong with the poet's 'prayer' (line 4), in his own opinion?

b) Do you think there is any connection between line 2 and line 6? If so, can you explain it?

24. *De Profundis* (1897)

Of course you had your illusions, lived in them indeed, and through their shifting mists and coloured veils saw all things changed. You thought, I remember quite well, that your devoting yourself to me, to the entire exclusion of your family and family life, was a proof of your wonderful appreciation of me, and your great affection. No doubt to you it seemed so. But recollect that with me was luxury, high living, unlimited pleasure, money without stint. Your family life bored you. The 'cold cheap wine of Salisbury', to use a phrase of your own making, was distasteful to you. On my side, and along with my intellectual attractions, were the fleshpots of Egypt. When you could not find me to be with, the companions whom you chose as substitutes were not flattering. (. . .)

I also had my illusions. I thought life was going to be a brilliant comedy, and that you were to be one of many graceful figures in it. I found it to be a revolting and repellent tragedy, and that the sinister occasion of the great catastrophe, sinister in its concentration of aim and intensity of narrowed will-power, was yourself, stripped of that mask of joy and pleasure by which you, no less than I, had been deceived and led astray.

Listening

This is part of another letter of Wilde's to Alfred Douglas, written from Reading Gaol in 1897.

While listening, make a note of what Wilde says were Douglas's likes and dislikes:

LIKES	DISLIKES
devotion to me	family and family life
luxury	....
....	....

Reading

a) According to Wilde, did Douglas appreciate and 'love' him? What alternatives were available to Douglas?

b) What was Wilde's first illusion?

c) Wilde's disillusionment returns to his conviction and sentence (after the third trial in 1895) to two years' imprisonment – 'the great catastrophe' (line 16). Try to explain the following phrases.

'concentration of aim' (line 16)
'intensity of narrowed will-power' (line 17)

It is important to bear in mind that, in 1895, the majority of English people were very shocked by Wilde's criminal trials.

d) Who was 'deceived and led astray' (line 19)? Why? And what caused it? Refer closely to the text to support your answers.

Discussion

e) Wilde mentions Douglas's 'mask of joy and pleasure'. Try to recall as many instances as you can in this programme where masks are worn or referred to. Is Wilde himself wearing a mask in *De Profundis*?

25. *The Ballad of Reading Gaol* (1898)

I never saw a man who looked
   With such a wistful eye
Upon that little tent of blue
   Which prisoners call the sky,
And at every drifting cloud that went
   With sails of silver by.

I walked, with other souls in pain,
   Within another ring,
And was wondering if the man had done
   A great or little thing,
When a voice behind me whispered low,
   'That fellow's got to swing.'

Dear Christ! The very prison walls
   Suddenly seemed to reel,
And the sky above my head became
   Like a casque of scorching steel;
And, though I was a soul in pain,
   My pain I could not feel.

I only knew what hunted thought
   Quickened his step, and why
He looked upon the garish day
   With such a wistful eye;
The man had killed the thing he loved,
   And so he had to die.

* * *

Yet each man kills the thing he loves,
   By each let this be heard,
Some do it with a bitter look,
   Some with a flattering word,
The coward does it with a kiss,
   The brave man with a sword!

Some kill their loves when they are young,
   And some when they are old;
Some strangle with the hands of Lust,

Some with the hands of Gold:
The kindest use a knife, because
The dead so soon grow cold.

Some love too little, some too long,
Some sell, and others buy;
Some do the deed with many tears,
And some without a sigh:
For each man kills the thing he loves,
Yet each man does not die.

Listening

A ballad is a poem or song which has a strong rhythm and regular rhymes. In this ballad, listen carefully to the 'music' of the verse. Which lines do you find particularly striking? Can you say why?

Reading

a) What is the 'man' (line 1) doing? What is the poet doing when he sees this man? Where do you think they are?
b) Match the words in the left-hand column with the definitions in the right-hand column.

wistful (line 2)	wave from side to side
drifting (line 5)	sexual desire
got to swing (line 12)	floating
reel (line 14)	very bright
casque (line 16)	must be hanged
hunted (line 19)	nostalgic; philosophical
garish (line 21)	hat of metal
Lust (line 33)	threatened (with death)

Discussion

c) How many variations and contrasts can you find in the last three verses (lines 25–42)? Do you think the 'killing' is always meant literally, i.e. the death of another person? Justify your answer by close reference to these three verses.
d) Do you ever get very angry? If so, who provokes you most – family, friends, other people you know or complete strangers?
e) Write one paragraph saying whether you agree or disagree with capital punishment, i.e. the killing by the state of serious criminals such as murderers.

26. *The Critic as Artist* (1890)

To be good, according to the vulgar standard of goodness, is obviously quite easy. It merely requires a certain amount of sordid terror, a certain lack of imaginative thought, and a certain low passion for middle-class respectability. Aesthetics are higher than ethics. They belong to a more spiritual sphere. To discern the beauty of a thing is the finest point to which we can arrive. Even a colour-sense is more important, in the development of the individual, than a sense of right and wrong. Aesthetics, in fact, are to ethics in the sphere of conscious civilization, what, in the sphere of the external world, sexual is to natural selection. Ethics, like natural selection, make existence possible. Aesthetics, like sexual selection, make life lovely and wonderful, fill it with new forms, and give it progress, and variety and change.

Listening

In this extract from an essay, pay particular attention during the first listening to words and phrases which indicate the things Wilde contrasts with 'the vulgar standard of goodness'.

Reading

a) Try to explain the connection Wilde is making between 'ethics' and being 'good'. Refer in particular to the second sentence of the passage.

b) According to Wilde, are the following things identified with aesthetics (A) or ethics (E)?

to be good (line 1)
middle-class respectability (line 4)
spiritual sphere (line 5)
beauty (line 5)
a colour-sense (line 6)
a sense of right and wrong (line 7)

Discussion

c) What is the difference between 'natural selection' and 'sexual selection'? Do these ideas come from 'the external world' or from 'conscious civilization'? Try to summarise what Wilde is saying.

A plan with the headings 'Mind', 'Body' and 'Social Behaviour' will probably help. And give your own opinions, too.

27. Letters to Robert Ross and Reginald Turner (1899)

It was a great pleasure writing your name on the page of dedication. I only wish it was a more wonderful work of art – of higher seriousness of intent – but it has some amusing things in it, and I think the tone and temper of the whole thing bright and happy.

It was extraordinary reading the play over. How I used to toy with that tiger Life! I hope you will find a place for me amongst your nicest books, not near anything by Hichens or George Moore. I should like it to be within speaking distance of *Dorian Gray*.

Listening

Both these letters were written early in 1899. As you listen, try to work out what event provoked Wilde to send the letters. Do you think anything else was included *with* the letters? If so, what might it have been?

Reading

a) Four years after its first theatrical production, do you think Wilde still likes his play?

b) Try to rewrite, in your own words, the second sentence of the second letter.

Discussion

c) Do you think Reginald Turner's bookshelves were carefully arranged? How about yours? Have you ever made a list of your books? Why? Or why not?

28. *The Importance of Being Earnest* (1895)

LADY BRACKNELL: You can take a seat, Mr Worthing.

JACK: Thank you, Lady Bracknell, I prefer standing.

LADY BRACKNELL: I feel bound to tell you that you are not down on my list of eligible young men, although I have the same list as the dear Duchess of Bolton has. We work together, in fact. However, I am quite ready to enter your name, should your answers be what a really affectionate mother requires. Do you smoke?

JACK: Well, yes, I must admit I smoke.

LADY BRACKNELL: I am glad to hear it. A man should always have an occupation of some kind. There are far too many idle men in London as it is. How old are you?

JACK: Twenty-nine.

LADY BRACKNELL: A very good age to be married at. I have always been of the opinion that a man who desires to get married should know either everything or nothing. Which do you know?

JACK: I know nothing, Lady Bracknell.

LADY BRACKNELL: I am pleased to hear it. I do not approve of anything that tampers with natural ignorance. Ignorance is like a delicate exotic fruit; touch it and the bloom is gone. The whole theory of modern education is radically unsound. Fortunately in England, at any rate, education produces no effect whatsoever. If it did, it would prove a serious danger to the upper classes, and probably lead to acts of violence in Grosvenor Square. What is your income?

JACK: Between seven and eight thousand a year.

LADY BRACKNELL: In land, or in investments?

JACK: In investments, chiefly.

LADY BRACKNELL: That is satisfactory. What between the duties expected of one during one's lifetime, and the duties exacted from one after one's death, land has ceased to be either a profit or a pleasure. It gives one position, and prevents one from keeping it up. That's all that can be said about land.

JACK: I have a country house with some land, of course, attached to it, about fifteen hundred acres, I believe; but I don't depend on that for my real income. In fact, as far as I can make out, the poachers are the only people who make anything out of it.

LADY BRACKNELL: A country house! How many bedrooms? Well, that point can be cleared up afterwards. You have a town house, I hope?

A girl with a simple, unspoiled nature, like Gwendolen, could hardly be expected to reside in the country.

JACK: Well, I own a house in Belgrave Square, but it is let by the year to Lady Bloxham. Of course, I can get it back whenever I like, at six months' notice.

LADY BRACKNELL: Lady Bloxham? I don't know her.

JACK: Oh, she goes about very little. She is a lady considerably advanced in years.

LADY BRACKNELL: Ah, nowadays that is no guarantee of respectability of character. What number in Belgrave Square?

JACK: 149.

LADY BRACKNELL: The unfashionable side. I thought there was something. However, that could easily be altered.

JACK: Do you mean the fashion, or the side?

LADY BRACKNELL: Both, if necessary, I presume. What are your politics?

JACK: Well, I am afraid I really have none. I am a Liberal Unionist.

LADY BRACKNELL: Oh, they count as Tories. They dine with us. Or come in the evening, at any rate. Now to minor matters. Are your parents living?

JACK: I have lost both my parents.

LADY BRACKNELL: To lose one parent, Mr Worthing, may be regarded as a misfortune; to lose both looks like carelessness. Who was your father? He was evidently a man of some wealth. Was he born in what the Radical papers call the purple of commerce, or did he rise from the ranks of the aristocracy?

JACK: I'm afraid I really don't know. The fact is, Lady Bracknell, I said I had lost my parents. It would be nearer the truth to say that my parents seem to have lost me. – I don't actually know who I am by birth. I was – well, I was found.

LADY BRACKNELL: Found!

JACK: The late Mr Thomas Cardew, an old gentleman of a very charitable and kindly disposition, found me, and gave me the name of Worthing, because he happened to have a first-class ticket for Worthing in his pocket at the time. Worthing is a place in Sussex. It is a seaside resort.

LADY BRACKNELL: Where did the charitable gentleman who had a first-class ticket for this seaside resort find you?

JACK: In a hand-bag.

LADY BRACKNELL: A hand-bag?

JACK: Yes, Lady Bracknell, I was in a hand-bag – a somewhat large, black leather hand-bag, with handles to it – an ordinary hand-bag, in fact.

LADY BRACKNELL: In what locality did this Mr James, or Thomas, Cardew come across this ordinary hand-bag?

JACK: In the cloak-room at Victoria Station. It was given to him in mistake for his own.

LADY BRACKNELL: The cloak-room at Victoria Station?

JACK: Yes. The Brighton line.

LADY BRACKNELL: The line is immaterial. Mr Worthing, I confess I feel somewhat bewildered by what you have just told me. To be born, or at any rate bred, in a hand-bag, whether it had handles or not, seems to me to display a contempt for the ordinary decencies of family life that reminds one of the worst excesses of the French Revolution. And I presume you know what that unfortunate movement led to? As for the particular locality in which the hand-bag was found, a cloak-room at a railway station might serve to conceal a social indiscretion – has probably, indeed, been used for that purpose before now – but it could hardly be regarded as an assured basis for a recognized position in good society.

JACK: May I ask you then what you would advise me to do? I need hardly say I would do anything in the world to ensure Gwendolen's happiness.

LADY BRACKNELL: I would strongly advise you, Mr Worthing, to try and acquire some relations as soon as possible, and to make a definite effort to produce at any rate one parent, of either sex, before the season is quite over.

JACK: Well, I don't see how I could possibly manage to do that. I can produce the hand-bag at any moment. It is in my dressing-room at home. I really think that should satisfy you, Lady Bracknell.

LADY BRACKNELL: Me, sir! What has it to do with me? You can hardly imagine that I and Lord Bracknell would dream of allowing our only daughter – a girl brought up with the utmost care – to marry into a cloak-room, and form an alliance with a parcel. Good morning, Mr Worthing!

Listening

Jack wants to marry Lady Bracknell's daughter, Gwendolen. Lady Bracknell has a notebook. This scene is often called 'the hand-bag scene'. It should be listened to for enjoyment. You might like to pick out some of Lady Bracknell's more eccentric views and opinions and decide if she really is a 'monster' (as Jack describes her immediately afterwards).

Reading

a) Look at the passage down to 'Are your parents living?' (lines 57–8). Lady Bracknell asks Jack questions on the following subjects. Try to put them into the same order as they occur in the scene.

> money – how much/where from?
> political opinions?
> residence?
> smoker?
> education?
> age?

If you were Lady Bracknell, what notes would you make?

b) Is Lady Bracknell totally satisfied by all Jack's answers up to this stage? Where, if anywhere, does she express doubts about his suitability as a son-in-law?

c) Can you explain why Lady Bracknell repeats Jack's words 'charitable gentleman', 'first-class ticket' and 'seaside resort' (lines 75–6)?

d) Lady Bracknell says, 'The line is immaterial' (line 87). Has the relationship between the two characters changed by this point? Can you say how, and why?

e) What kind of 'social indiscretion' (line 95) may Lady Bracknell be referring to, do you think?

Discussion

f) Write Jack's entry in his diary for the day of this interview. Then write a short letter from Lady Bracknell to the Duchess of Bolton (see line 5) giving your opinions on Jack Worthing's suitability as a husband.

g) Do you think it is a good idea for parents to choose marriage partners for their children? What advantages can you see?

The Victorian poet, Alfred, Lord Tennyson, wrote, 'In the spring a young man's fancy lightly turns to thoughts of love'. Do you agree that there is a 'season' for love, as in the nineteenth-century concept of '*the* season' (April to June), when eligible young men and women were introduced to each other at parties organized by their parents?

29. *Epilogue*

GERALD: I suppose society is wonderfully delightful!
LORD ILLINGWORTH: To be in it is merely a bore. But to be out of it simply a tragedy.

(*A Woman of No Importance*)

Never speak disrespectfully of Society, Algernon. Only people who can't get into it do that.

(*The Importance of Being Earnest*)

All art is at once surface and symbol. Those who go beneath the surface do so at their peril. Those who read the symbol do so at their peril.

(Preface to *The Picture of Dorian Gray*)

Would you like to know the great drama of my life? – It's that I've put my genius into my life; I've put only my talent into my works.

(attributed)

LORD ILLINGWORTH: The Book of Life begins with a man and a woman in a garden.
MRS ARBUTHNOT: It ends with Revelations.

(*A Woman of No Importance*)

It would really be more than the English could stand, if another century began and I were still alive.

(attributed)

I am dying above my means.

(attributed)

Yet all is well; he has but passed
    To Life's appointed bourne:
And alien tears will fill for him
    Pity's long-broken urn,
For his mourners will be outcast men,
    And outcasts always mourn.

(*The Ballad of Reading Gaol*)

Listening

Can you find any puns, paradoxes, contradictions or epigrams in these closing quotations?

Discussion

a) What does 'Society' mean? Would you like to be 'in' society?

b) Oscar Wilde lived in England for nearly thirty years, but he was Irish. The six and seventh quotations here date from when he was dying in November 1900, penniless, in Paris. He was only forty-six years old.

The phrase 'living above one's means' indicates a life-style which is more expensive than someone can afford. Do you find Wilde's dying phrase funny or pathetic?

c) Wilde is buried in Paris. The last verse here is carved on his tomb. 'Outcasts' (line 6) means rejected people – rejected by 'society' perhaps. Wilde did not write this verse about himself, but do you think it is appropriate?

d) Do you prefer the following verse, which Oscar Wilde certainly knew, and which may have inspired him? Why, or why not?

A thousand Powers keep religious state,
In water, fiery realm, and airy bourne;
And silent as a consecrated urn,
Hold sphery sessions for a season due.
Yet few of these far majesties, ah, few!
Have bared their operations to this globe.

In your opinion would this verse have been a better epitaph for Oscar Wilde?

Final listening

Now that you have followed the whole programme through, which performances and texts do you remember with most enjoyment?

Were there any you didn't like at all? Discuss why, comparing them with texts you did enjoy.

Performance

You might want to try performing some of the texts. You can do this just by using one or more voices, and interpreting the characters and roles, or by *acting out* some scenes in front of the class.

There is no need to imitate the voices on the cassette. Try other interpretations and ways of speaking, to see how they influence the interpretation and the performance.

The Author: Oscar Wilde

Oscar Wilde was born in Dublin, Ireland, in 1854 and died in Paris, France, in 1900. He was a very successful student at Trinity College, Dublin (1871–4), and Magdalen College, Oxford (1874–8). He became well known in London after his graduation from Oxford University. He believed in the artistic teachings of the English 'Aesthetes', whose inspiration came to a large extent from the French 'Symbolistes'. At the beginning of his literary career Wilde wrote a lot of poetry (collected in the volume called *Poems*, 1881) and two unsuccessful plays. He also went to the United States and gave lectures for about a year. He got married in 1884. At this time he earned his living as a journalist. Between 1887 and 1890 he wrote many stories. The last – and longest – of these stories, *The Picture of Dorian Gray*, caused a controversy in 1890, because it did not condemn its hero's bad deeds. Many people thought that Dorian Gray was homosexual, and that he was a corrupting influence on the people he met. Many people also thought that Oscar Wilde himself was homosexual. Wilde revised the story, adding several chapters and a preface; the novel of *Dorian Gray* was published in 1891. Many of Wilde's earlier works were also published in 1891, and one of his early plays was given its first production.

Wilde achieved fame through notoriety. His fame prompted George Alexander, a London theatre manager, to invite Oscar to write a play for him. Between 1891 and 1894 Wilde wrote four comedies. They were widely considered the most brilliant comedies in English since Congreve (whose plays were first produced between 1693 and 1700). Wilde also wrote a short play in French, *Salomé*.

Oscar Wilde was sent to prison for two years in 1895. He foolishly argued with the Marquess of Queensbury, father of Wilde's friend Lord Alfred Douglas, when Queensbury accused him of homosexual behaviour. There was a lot of evidence that Wilde had been having homosexual relationships with younger men for many years.

Towards the end of his prison sentence, Wilde wrote a very long letter to Alfred Douglas. Wilde's literary manager called this letter *De Profundis*. After Wilde was released from prison, in 1897, his only new work was a long poem based upon his prison experiences, called *The Ballad of Reading Gaol*. He never returned to England, and died in Paris $3\frac{1}{2}$ years after his release from Reading. He was only forty-six years old.

The works of Oscar Wilde

Poetry

Critics pay little attention to Wilde's poetry. His earliest poems were published in Dublin in the 1870s, and he continued to send poems to Irish publishers while he was in Oxford (1874–8). His greatest success as a poet came in 1878, when *Ravenna* won the Oxford University Poetry Prize.

One of Wilde's earliest publications was *Poems*, which came out in 1881. He revised all his earlier work and added many previously unpublished poems. He rarely attempted poetry again, although his play *The Duchess of Padua*, written in 1882–3, is in verse. He published a long poem called *The Harlot's House* in 1885. A poem called *The Sphinx* was probably completed in 1883, but was not published until 1894. *The Ballad of Reading Gaol* was first published in 1898.

Prose works

Wilde wrote an enormous number of articles for London newspapers, which are now lost. He also wrote many letters, the majority of which are no longer available in print. But he also wrote essays and stories.

Four of the most important essays were collected in the volume called *Intentions*, published in 1891. *The Soul of Man Under Socialism* was published earlier in the same year.

The Canterville Ghost was the first of Wilde's stories to be published, in 1887. Two collections were published in 1891. Earlier works which were not collected and reprinted in that year were *The Happy Prince and Other Stories* (five stories published in 1888) and *The Portrait of Mr W.H.* (published in 1889). *The Picture of Dorian Gray* was first published in June 1890; Wilde added six chapters and a preface before its publication in book form in April 1891.

Drama

Wilde's literary reputation rests principally upon four comedies written in the 1890s. These are (with dates of first production): *Lady Windermere's Fan* (1892), *A Woman of No Importance* (1893), *An Ideal Husband* (1895) and *The Importance of Being Earnest* (1895).

Wilde also wrote two plays in the 1880s. Both received their first productions in New York. *Vera* was published in London in 1880, and produced in New York in 1883. *The Duchess of Padua*, a play in verse, was published in 1883. It was produced in New York in 1891. Both plays were unsuccessful, and are largely forgotten nowadays.

In 1891–2 Wilde decided to write a play in French. *Salomé* was completed in 1892, and a production was mounted in London but never took place. The play was published in French in 1893, and in an English translation by Lord Alfred Douglas in 1894. The original text was first produced in Paris in 1896, when Wilde was in prison. (The play is best remembered now because it was turned into an opera by Richard Strauss in 1905.)

Itineraries

After a first reading and listening to the complete performance of *Oscar: The Importance of Being Wilde*, you may find it easier to work in greater detail on small groups of texts. This can be done quite simply in sections: the first five texts, the next five, and so on. Alternatively, you may wish to concentrate on texts which have close thematic or stylistic links. Some suggestions are:

Death
Requiescat (3), Sonnet on Hearing the Dies Irae ... (8), *The Ballad of Reading Gaol* (25).

Witty aristocrats
The Picture of Dorian Gray (second passage) (6), *A Woman of No Importance* (second passage) (17), *The Importance of Being Earnest* (first passage) (18), transcript of the first trial (22).

Horror/melodrama
The Canterville Ghost (11), Fabien dei Franchi (12), *The Picture of Dorian Gray* (third passage) (19).

Sonnets
Sonnet, On Hearing the Dies Irae ... (8), Fabien dei Franchi (12), Sonnet to Liberty (16), Taedium Vitae (20).

Essays/argument/Aestheticism
Quotations (1), The Decay of Lying (2), The Truth of Masks (5), The Soul of Man Under Socialism (15), The Critic as Artist (26), Epilogue (29).

Also, the dramatic scenes – from *Lady Windermere's Fan* (14), *A Woman of No Importance* (10, 17), *An Ideal Husband* (7) and *The Importance of Being Earnest* (18, 28) – may be read as a 'text group'. Many other combinations of selected texts are possible.

Glossary

Meanings are given only for the contexts in which the words are found. Meanings of words included in the vocabulary exercises are not given here.

absurdly   ridiculously
acre   a land measure; slightly under half a hectare
admit   agree, with reluctance
adopt   assume, take on
affectation   social pretension or pretentiousness
agony   pain and suffering
aim   purpose
ajar   slightly open
alien   belonging to strangers or foreigners
alliance   partnership
allow (of)   permit
alluding   making reference
aloof   at a distance, unconcerned
apart from   without reference to
appointed   decided, decreed
archaistic   showing an interest in the past
august   grand, noble

barricades   obstacles built by political revolutionaries
base   worthless, without value
bewildered   taken aback, very surprised
bid you good-bye   say farewell to you
bidding   command
bloom   ripeness, perfection
Book of Life   the Holy Bible of Christianity
bound   obliged
bourne   boundary, limit, (poetically) a final resting-place
branded   burnt
bred   raised, brought up as a child
broke off   ended, terminated (an engagement to be married)
burnished   applied like a coating of gold

candidly honestly

cannonades making war (literally, firing cannons)

catastrophe disaster

chill cold, freezing

civilized acceptably refined, pleasant

clever intelligent

cloak-room left luggage office (now obsolete)

coffin-board the wood used to make a coffin

come across find

compromise relaxation of strongly held feelings (to accommodate a different point of view)

conduce (to) encourage

confirmed resolute, not changing

consoled made to feel happier

crumbs small pieces of bread

cultivate develop, to make grow

curious odd, unusual

darted hurried, rushed

decent respectable, morally acceptable

declaring proclaiming, saying in a forthright manner

decline refuse, reject

demoralizing discouraging

discern see and recognize

discreet showing discernment, cautious

diplomatic career work abroad

disarmed taken aback, unsettled (literally, deprived of weapons)

dissonant without harmony

duel fight (possibly with swords or guns) between two people

earnestness solemnity, the lack of a sense of humour

effective dramatic, impressive

eligible worthy of being chosen (for marriage)

else otherwise

empurpled changed to a purple colour; (of vines) mature

evident clear, obvious

exacted demanded, solicited (as an obligation)

excuse reason (for negative behaviour)

expectations prospects (of wealth)

fearful terrible, appalling

filch rob, plunder

finds you out   discovers your secret

fit   suitable

flattering   praising immoderately

fleshpots   brothels, bordellos

folio   book (of a particular size); the first published collection of Shakespeare's plays was printed in a 'folio' edition in 1623

folly   foolishness

(to be) fond   like

forte   strongest personal accomplishment or ability

frenzied   mad

frets   moves anxiously

gaudy   brightly coloured

gilt   covered in gold

glade   small group of trees

gleaner   person who picks up grain

glided   moved silently

go on   continue

gore   blood, or exposed flesh

graceful   elegant and attractive

guardian   person appointed by a court of law to look after the upbringing of a child

gutter   drain or depression at the side of a road

hangings   curtains surrounding an old-fashioned (four-poster) bed

hard   (*The Picture of Dorian Gray*) severe

hard   (*The Canterville Ghost*) rapidly

hard and fast   (*Lady Windermere's Fan*) rigidly fixed

hardly   (*The Importance of Being Earnest*) not really, barely

harm   damage

hideous   vile, terrible

hind   farm worker (now obsolete)

illusions   mistaken ideas

immaterial   without relevance

immensely   very much

implored   begged

incarnation   bringing to physical reality

insolent   lacking respect

intensely   very much

invalid   chronically ill person

invaluable   extremely valuable

invariably   without exception

investments   money paid as interest in return for subscriptions to the financial capital of a company

inviolate   which demand respect

knout   punishment (literally, flogging with a whip)

lackeyed groom   poor servant

laid up   being ill and suffering in bed

leaden   made of lead

left   remaining

let   rented

Liberal Unionist   supporter of the section of the British Liberal party which (in the 1890s) wished to keep Ireland as part of the United Kingdom. The 'Tories' (the Conservative party) all supported the Union of Great Britain and Ireland.

livery   the costume of a servant

loathsome of visage   with a horrible face

locality   place

longing   intense desire

lowliest   most humble, poorest

lure   attract, entice, seduce

lyre   ancient musical instrument

marvel   cause of happy surprise

match-girl   girl who sells matches

meanest   poorest, least valued

mercenary   attracted by money

mesh   mix, mingle

mock   denigrate, laugh at

monstrous soul-life   inhuman mental anguish

mourners   people who grieve another person's death

myth   fiction, untrue saying

nicest   most pleasant

notice   advance warning

objection   adverse or contrary opinion

outcast(s)   rejected, reviled (people)

over   past

paltry   insignificant (literally, ragged)

paramour   lover

phantom   ghost

pluck out   remove

poachers   people who steal birds and animals from privately owned land

portico   porch, entrance to a building

practically   in realistic terms

pre-Raphaelite   agreeing with a nineteenth-century artistic movement in Britain which followed pre-Renaissance ideals (dating back before the birth of the Italian painter Raffaello Sanzio – known as Raphael – in 1483)

profess   claim

proper   morally pure and acceptable

provincial   outside the capital (London)

Puritan   person with strict ideas about morality

purple of commerce   rapidly expanding (and profitable) world of business (the colour purple is associated with royalty and riches)

put down   forbidden, repressed

radically   completely, absolutely

rather   instead

reap   cut down

recollect   remember

recreant   rebellious but cowardly

repellent   disgusting

resolved   decided

resort   place for holidays

revives   brings back to life

romance   sentimental relationship

ruined   destroyed

salon   room for receiving guests; also the company which assembles at upper-class parties, for which the hostess usually claimed credit (this is a very out-of-date idea now)

save   except

scandalous   outrageous, socially unacceptable

scene   argument, disagreement

scrapes   accidents, unfortunate adventures

(the) season   period of the year when matchmaking was carried out in 'high society'

seized   grabbed, picked up violently

sent down   (at formal dinners) instructed to leave the dining-room

set themselves   decided that their role is

(in the) shade   out of the sunlight

shame   disgrace

sheaves   bundles of ripe corn, wheat, etc.

shifting   moving

shrill   noisy, with a high-pitched sound

sinister   disturbingly unpleasant

slanderous   insulting, ill-spoken

sneered   made noises to show a lack of concern

sojourn   live, dwell (perhaps on a temporary basis)

sordid   dirty, filthy

sores   wounds, unpleasantness

stand   tolerate

stand up for   support

starve   go without food

stern   strict, not showing tenderness

stifled   quiet, restrained

stint   limit, restraint

strife   discord, noisy disagreement

stripped   deprived (literally, of clothing)

suggestive   provoking contemplation

surrender   give up

swooped   descended quickly (in the air)

symbol   a representation of something abstract, often in visual terms

tainted   discoloured, made bitter

tarnished   spoiled, made dull

temper   mood

third-rate   low-class

thistledown   feathery growth on a mature thistle (most of which bears seeds and is carried by the wind)

thoroughly   completely

twilight   dusk, the end of the day

unsound   wrong, misconceived

uphold   support

utmost   greatest

utterly   completely

vain   proud, admiring oneself

vainly   without success

veils   semi-transparent fabrics, fine nets or gauzes

vex worry
vice evil habit
voilà tout (French) that is all
vulgar common and despicable

wainscoting wooden wall-panels
want deprivation, poverty
will-power intellectual force
woe misery, despair
wringing squeezing

yet nevertheless
yielded succumbed, gave way

Answers

Many of the tasks and exercises do not have 'right' or 'wrong' answers. Nevertheless, guidance is given here to all the activities.

Where there is a definite 'right answer', this is given. Frequently, however, you will find a suggested response, which is not intended to be a complete answer. For exercises which involve rewriting the author's words, help is usually given in the exercises themselves; in such cases, we have simply put 'Rewriting' in these notes.

A large proportion of tasks depend entirely upon your interpretation of, and reaction to the text, and in these cases we have used the word 'Open' to mean it's up to you!

1. *Quotations* (p. 14)

Listening: Open.

a) If you 'declare' something to a customs officer when arriving in a foreign country, this means you believe that you may be required to pay tax for something you are bringing with you to that country. In its simpler sense, 'to declare' means to make a statement, often in a dramatic manner.

b) Suggested response: 'In a commentary based upon the perception of beautiful things, (the writer's) point of view is the be all and end all.' This attempt at rewriting shows that Wilde's original brief phrase (six words only) may be regarded as an epigram – see below.

c) Open. Reference to more than one dictionary is recommended. Masks cover a person's face, so cannot be true, but perhaps the face does not reveal the person's true character, so this title is both a contradiction and a paradox. The word 'declare' – see (a) above – is the only pun in these introductory quotations. The concise, witty and thought-provoking nature

of these statements means that they can all be classified as epigrams.
d) Open.

e) Suggested response: experience means being changed by meeting something previously unknown or misunderstood. It might be interesting again to compare the definitions in two or more English dictionaries. 'Experience' can be pleasant or unpleasant; the phrase implies that unpleasantness probably causes this change.

2. *The Decay of Lying* (p. 16)

Above all, according to Wilde, Art expresses nothing but 'itself'. It usually does *not* express the spirit of the age in which it is created. Bad art is derived from 'life and Nature'. See a).

a) All the statements are true, but only up to a point. 'Not necessarily' and 'usually' indicate that Wilde is not prepared to say that these characteristics are 'always' or 'never' present.

b) Open. Life and Nature should not be rejected but somehow transformed with the help of the artist's imagination. Rewriting.

c) 'Suggestive' implies the inspiration of the artist. Twilight or the moon have often inspired the work of artists. Were you inspired?

The paradox is that the loveliness of twilight is, in itself, less 'useful' than the inspiration it has given to poets – poetry is more valuable than nature, according to Wilde.

3. *Requiescat* (p. 18)

A woman or girl ('she' repeated several times) has died and been buried. Many words suggest or confirm this: some examples might be 'under' (line 2), 'dust' (line 8), 'coffin' (line 13). There are many more.

a) He seems to be speaking to other people who are mourning the woman's death; but he is 'alone' (line 15) – perhaps he is speaking to himself.

b) The poet was obviously very closely attached to the dead woman – 'All my life' – (line 19). Many critics think that Oscar Wilde was remembering the death of his younger sister, Isola, in February 1867, when she was nine years old. (Oscar was then twelve.)

c) 'Lyre and sonnet' (line 18); the pleasures of music and poetry are denied to the dead woman. 'Earth', in the final line, is a striking contrast, but others exist in the poem.

d) Open.

4. *The Picture of Dorian Gray* (p. 20)

Listening: Open.
a) Open. Dorian implies an uncaring attitude towards the past; in the future, he hopes to master and enjoy his emotions.
b) Dorian says to Basil, 'You only taught me to be vain.' Presumably, Harry taught Dorian something more – see text 6. Basil identified Dorian as 'a wonderful boy' – simple, natural, affectionate and unspoiled. Final response: open.
c) In order: 3 – 'It is not a disaster'; 1 – 'Actors and actresses'; 4 – 'Most actors'; 6 – 'She was not like that'; 2 – 'On her final appearance'; 7 – 'When she knew'; 5 – 'Her self-sacrifice'.
d) Open.

5. *The Truth of Masks* (p 22)

The mood is basically pessimistic; important words include 'pity', 'attack', 'higher qualifications'.
a) Some suggestions: they have formed their opinions prematurely; they place an exaggerated importance on great acting from the past; they fail to recognise 'beauty'.
b) Open.

6 *The Picture of Dorian Gray* (p. 23)

Sir Henry praises Dorian Gray's youth and beauty. Many contrasting words can be found. Time is denoted by the following words: 'any longer', 'never', 'your days', 'our age', 'new', 'always', 'for ever', 'longer' – plus, of course, all the words which contrast youth with age.
a) Parker is the butler, the most senior servant in aristocratic nineteenth-century English homes. Sir Henry says that Dorian should 'sit in the shade' – out of the sun. In his opinion a suntan would not be attractive: 'spoiled', 'never paint you again', 'unbecoming' – these words and phrases all demonstrate Sir Henry's opinion.
b) In order: very bright light; making less beautiful; cut; horrible, foul; enjoy, make the best of; spend extravagantly; shake with horror; romantic game, affair.

c) Rewriting. Open.

d) 'Always'.

e) Open.

7. *An Ideal Husband* (p. 25)

The speakers are Mrs Cheveley and Lord Goring (always called 'Arthur' by her, although he never uses her first name). The Chilterns – Sir Robert and Lady Gertrude Chiltern – are the only other characters named. Mrs Cheveley mentions two former husbands, but not their names. 'That is my offer' (line 16/17) is the 'turning-point' of the scene, when business becomes more important than romance.

a) Open. Lord Goring probably did love Mrs Cheveley, as he does not deny her assertion and agrees that, with time, a man's love for a woman dies. Neither character now loves the other. Arthur's feelings are clear from the above; Mrs Cheveley uses the verb form 'did love' to emphasize that any love she felt is now past.

b) She wants Lord Goring to marry her. She offers him a letter written by his best friend, Sir Robert Chiltern, which – if made public – would destroy Sir Robert's political career.

c) At least two, who were 'bad'. There is no evidence in the passage that she had more husbands who were good. Lord Goring is perhaps tempted to marry Mrs Cheveley by the chance of saving Sir Robert's reputation, but he quickly rejects her proposal. 'The Book of Numbers' may imply contempt for the instability of Mrs Cheveley's marriages, of which two at least are finished.

d) Mrs Cheveley is a blackmailer and a divorcee; most people would say she is a scoundrel, and probably a snob because she wants to become Lady Goring. She perhaps thinks she is a diplomat, but her 'work' overseas is unofficial and almost certainly illegal. She shows signs of sentimentality, but she is not a sentimentalist. Lord Goring is an aristocrat and a wit; he may be a diplomat and/or a snob, but there is no evidence in the passage.

Neither character is a defender, foreigner, ignoramus, sentimentalist or tragedian. Defender (unless qualified by other words) applies only to the world of sport. Foreigner applies only to a person born and raised abroad, and not to someone who has simply lived abroad for a time. An ignoramus is a stupid person – not someone who is unaware of one or two facts. Sentimentalist applies to someone whose behaviour is guided principally by the 'softer' emotions, such as affection, sympathy, pity, indulgence, etc. – usually excessively so. Tragedians exist only in the performing arts, principally the theatre: they are writers of tragic dramas, or actors who specialize in tragic roles.

e) Open.

f) Open. Sir Robert revealed confidential government information which enabled a friend to make a lot of money on the Stock Exchange.

8. *Sonnet. On Hearing the Dies Irae Sung in the Sistine Chapel* (p. 28)

Listening: Open.

a) *a / b / b / a / a / c / c / a / d / e / f / d / e / f*. Open.

b) Line 4.

c) Rewriting. Wilde objects because he sees that nature expresses the idea of death more eloquently.

d) 'Thy' (line 3 and line 14), 'Thee' (line 5 and line 8). 'One who had no place of rest' (line 7) probably refers to Jesus Christ.

e) Open.

9. *The Happy Prince* (p. 29)

Listening: Open.

a) A ruby and a sapphire; 'next spring'. The sapphire (blue) is much more likely than the ruby (red).

b) 'You are blind now'; '*he loved him too well*'.

c) Rewriting. The cold weather causes the death of the swallow, but is probably not the real reason for the statue's broken heart.

10. *A Woman of No Importance* (p. 31)

Mrs Arbuthnot's attitude does not change. Lord Illingworth is trying to persuade her to agree to something she is opposed to: namely, that Gerald 'go away' with him. His argument begins in rational terms, then appeals to sentiment (with references to his parents), and ends in irritation, where Lord Illingworth seems close to abusing Mrs Arbuthnot.

a) He is 'over twenty years' but probably not *much* over. Lord Illingworth wants Gerald to 'go away' with him, and possibly perform some secretarial duties.

b) The mother wanted to give Mrs Arbuthnot money; the father tried to persuade Lord Illingworth to marry her. Mrs Arbuthnot rejected the mother's money, and agreed with the father.

c) Open. The repetition of 'my son' emphasizes that she alone has been responsible for Gerald's upbringing. Open; it is implied that Gerald will, in the future, encounter 'suffering and shame' because his mother was unmarried.

d) Yes. He is attracted by Lord Illingworth's offer of employment, which is more interesting than his work in a 'Provincial Bank'.

e) Open.

11. *The Canterville Ghost* (p. 34)

Listening: Open. The tone of the passage is humorous, not serious.

a) The Ghost appeared to Lady Barbara Modish in the disguise of 'Reckless Rupert', and she refused to marry into the Canterville family. This was a success for the Ghost, because both Lady Barbara and her lover, Jack Castletown, died as a result of his appearance; they too became ghosts.

b) He appeared through the wooden panelling on the walls ('the wainscoting') and moved quietly along the corridor. The twins occupied 'the Blue Bed Chamber'; the 'hangings', or curtains – which may have covered the window or the walls, or surrounded an old-fashioned four-poster bed – were blue.

c) Two. One. His head.

d) Open. No words are spoken; only 'stifled shrieks of laughter'.

e) Open.

12. 'Fabien dei Franchi' (p. 36).

He is an actor. Lear, Romeo and Richard are the principal male roles in Shakespeare's plays *King Lear*, *Romeo and Juliet* and *Richard the Third*.
a) 'These things' are the dramatic scenes referred to in lines 1–7; 'thou' is the actor Fabien dei Franchi, who has acted roles in plays with scenes such as these.
b) Rewriting. Open.
c) Open.

13. 'The Portrait of Mr W.H.' (p. 38)

He was a beautiful actor called Willie Hughes, who influenced Shakespeare, and therefore (although this is not in the passage) was a teenager around the time the sonnets were written (at the end of the sixteenth century).
a) Rewriting.
b) Open. Shakespeare himself.
c) In order: T; T; F; T; F.
d) That Willie Hughes inspired Shakespeare to write the sonnets; the theory was originated by Cyril Graham.
e) Open.

14. *Lady Windermere's Fan* (p. 40)

No; she says, 'I should be sorry to be on the same level as an age like this.' Other comments also show her opposition to contemporary values.
a) Rewriting. Suggested response: Yes. People today appear to consider life as a financial gamble. It is not a gamble. It is a solemn pledge. Its goal is love. Its perfection is surrender/subjection.
b) Open.
c) Open. Her long first speech suggests that her upbringing was very important.
d) Open.

15. *The Soul of Man Under Socialism* (p. 42)

'Affected' is the judgement of 'the majority' on people like Wilde; 'selfish' is their judgement of the majority.
a) 'One's neighbour' who is likely to be part of 'the majority'.
b) and c) Open.

16. *Sonnet to Liberty* (p. 43)

'Roar' (line 4); 'rage' (line 7); 'dissonant cries' (line 8); 'bloody knout' (line 10); 'cannonades' (line 10). Many other words suggest violence. Apart from 'Liberty' itself (line 7), the other words most directly associated with the title are 'Democracies' (line 4), 'rights inviolate' (line 11) and possibly 'barricades' (line 13).
a) No; their eyes are 'dull', their 'woe' is 'unlovely', their 'minds' are ignorant and lacking in curiosity.
b) The thought is that 'kings' may deprive other countries of their sovereignty, and that the poet will not care.
c), d) and e) Open.

17. *A Woman of No Importance* (p. 44)

Some words might be: 'sad', 'ruining', 'uneducated', 'sufferings', 'poor', 'vice', 'sores', 'slavery', 'slaves'.
a) Open. Mr Cardew may be a politician; the Prime Minister even.
b) Open. He apparently recognizes that social deprivation exists there.
c) The final speech implies that he disagrees with current policy towards solving the problem, because it serves only to make the East Enders more content with their deprived status. Open. Being impartial/disinterested/uncaring.

18. *The Importance of Being Earnest* (p. 46)

They are obviously friends. Jack says later in the play that he is twenty-nine. At the end of the play, it emerges that Algernon is Jack's younger brother.

a) No; Algernon's first three words invite Jack to continue a conversation which has already begun.

b) Yes; his comments on 'high moral tone' and 'duty' indicate this. Rewriting. Ernest does not exist, but Jack would like to be as carefree as Algernon, and enjoys being in London. The misfortunes of his fictitious brother enable Jack to come to London from his home in the country.

c) The journalists 'haven't been at a University'. By referring to this, Algernon indicates that Jack *has*. 'So well' implies that Algernon approves of literary journalism, but he is probably being ironic, and not stating his true opinion.

d) To tell Jack the 'rules' of being a 'Bunburyist'; to avoid an unwelcome obligation to go to a dinner party organized by his Aunt Augusta.

e) Open. He implies that Mary Farquhar's behaviour draws attention to her happy marriage, which many people (including himself) do not wish to know about, perhaps because scandal is a more interesting topic for conversation.

f) Algernon is certainly not 'earnest'. Open.

19. *The Picture of Dorian Gray* (p. 48).

Listening: Open. Suggested words of violence and suspense may include: 'knife', 'stabbed', 'stain', 'glistened', 'killed' and many many more.

a) He was stabbed to death by Dorian Gray. (It is interesting to note that Dorian sees the knife rather than himself as the murderer.)

b) In order to free himself from the past; his present 'soul-life' is tormented by memories which 'warn' him of future torments. (His 'soul-life' is represented in the picture, which now shows a hideous old man, while Dorian himself still looks young and beautiful – but this is not revealed in the passage.)

c) They are *not* convulsive, efficient, observant, resplendent or scornful. Only Mrs Leaf may be described as delirious. So they were agitated, apprehensive, partly dressed, sleepy, talkative and terrified. The two passing gentlemen were observant and scornful.

d) Three (the two gentlemen – one of whom was Sir Henry Ashton's uncle – and a police constable). The gentlemen pass by; the constable attempts to enter the house, but then stands in another doorway to observe events. Three people enter the room: Francis, the coachman and one of the footmen.

e) Rewriting.

f) Open.

20. *Taedium Vitae* (p. 50)

'Stab', 'youth' and 'knives', all in line 1, are obvious links. There is no obvious connection in the subject matter, though the last word of the poem – 'sin' – does show an important link.

a) In order: line 2, line 4, line 5, line 1, line 3.

b) Open. He appears to give them very little importance.

c) Open. The poet says they are people who 'mock my life/ Knowing me not'. They may perhaps be people such as literary critics and false friends, whom Oscar Wilde always disliked.

d) No; he prefers 'the lowliest roof' (line 11). 'Strife' is what he most wants to avoid.

e) Open.

21. Letter to Lord Alfred Douglas (p. 51)

a) and b) Open.

22. Transcript of the First Trial (p. 52)

Preliminary: Open. Wilde appears to consider himself intellectually superior to Carson.

a) (to be) fond; liked.

b) Rewriting. Suggested response: Your questioning is irrelevant; as irrelevant as asking me whether the works of Shakespeare are morally acceptable.

c) Open.

d) Open. Carson is 'glad' because he dislikes Oscar Wilde, who is an 'artist', and does not want to be like him.

23. *Panthea* (p. 53)

The following words all relate to religion: 'guilt', 'temple', 'prayer', 'God' (of course!), 'heaven' – and perhaps also 'love'.

a) It is 'unanswered', although 'right'. Ultimately, therefore, the prayer is useless.

b) Open. 'Pleasure' (line 2) may be equated with 'One fiery-coloured moment' (line 6), and 'paramour' (line 2) with 'one great love' (line 6). A connection is clearly intended, the 'despair' of line 2 becoming the death of line 6.

24. *De Profundis* (p. 54)

Wilde says that Douglas liked everything which he, Oscar, could offer. (The 'fleshpots of Egypt' is a figure of speech.) 'Salisbury' refers to the home of Douglas's divorced mother; his dislikes, according to Wilde, were all towards Douglas's own family. The last sentence refers to Douglas's hatred of his father, which made him advise Oscar to begin the legal process which ruined him.

a) Probably not, because Douglas 'lived in' his 'illusions' – therefore Douglas's devotion was false, showing neither appreciation nor love. The alternatives were 'family life' and 'the fleshpots of Egypt' (i.e. sordid brothels).

b) He optimistically viewed life as happy and charming.

c) Suggested responses: determination to achieve a fixed purpose; forceful demonstration of the strength of ignorance. Wilde refers to the mentality of his prosecutors, and then says that Douglas was the cause of these feelings.

d) Both Wilde and Douglas – 'you, no less than I'. The main cause was Douglas's 'mask of joy and pleasure'; both men believed that this was genuine, not a 'mask', but Wilde now says that Douglas's real character is similar to that of his prosecutors at the trials. Other examples of Douglas's self-deception can be found in the first paragraph.

e) Open. Section 5 and the final quotation in section 1 will probably come to mind. There are many other examples. It can be argued that, in *De Profundis*, Wilde is wearing the mask of bitterness and suffering. (Four months after his release from prison he was living again with Douglas, in Naples.)

25. *The Ballad of Reading Gaol* (p. 56)

Listening: Open.

a) He is looking at the sky. The poet is walking with other people. They are all prisoners. Open; the 'man' is probably looking out of the window of a cell, which overlooks a prison yard where the poet and others are taking exercise.

b) In order: nostalgic, philosophical; floating; must be hanged; waved from side to side; hat of metal; threatened (with death); very bright; sexual desire.

c), d) and e) Open.

26. *The Critic as Artist* (p. 58)

Listening: The key word is 'aesthetics'. 'A more spiritual sphere', 'the beauty of a thing', 'the finest point', 'even a colour-sense' – all these phrases are used to emphasise Wilde's argument, as is the concluding sentence.

a) Rewriting.

b) In order: E / E / A / A / A / E.

c) Open. 'Natural selection' and 'sexual selection' are terms from Charles Darwin's studies of 'the external world' in *On the Origin of Species* (1859). 'Natural selection' is the preservation and continuation of species which are best adapted to their environment; 'sexual selection' is similar, but based on the abilities of species to reproduce themselves.

27. Letters to Robert Ross and Reginald Turner (p. 59)

Wilde appears happy (unusual in the year before his death). *The Importance of Being Earnest* had just been published for the first time. These letters accompanied copies of the printed text of his play to his two friends. 'The page of dedication' and 'a place for me amongst your nicest books' should indicate that the book of *The Importance* ... was included with these letters.

a) Yes; he considers it 'amusing' and 'bright and happy', even if he wishes it were more wonderful and serious.

b) Open. Suggested response: I used to make fun of life, which is really dangerous as a tiger.

c) Wilde implies that they were. Open.

28. *The Importance of Being Earnest* (p. 60)

Listening: Open.

a) In order: smoker; age; education; money – how much/where from; residence; political opinions/ Open.

b) Open. She seems less than fully satisfied about the character of Jack's tenant (Lady Bloxham) and the Belgrave Square address, and is perhaps disappointed that Jack is not a Tory. Otherwise she seems very happy with Jack's responses.

c) She is probably expressing both surprise and disgust at Jack's unlikely origins.

d) Open.

e) She probably means the abandoning of an unwanted, possibly illegitimate, child.

f) and g) Open.

29. Epilogue (p. 64)

Listening: Open. The only pun is 'Revelations'. The first attributed saying and the verse from *The Ballad of Reading Gaol* contain none of these features, but there are many examples in the other quotations.

a), b) and c) Open.

d) Open. The lines are taken from the epic poem *Endymion* (1818) by John Keats (Book 3, lines 30–35).